GW00750223

IMAGES *of Sport*

PLYMOUTH SPEEDWAY

OFFICIAL PROGRAMME   Price 3d.

PLYMOUTH SPEEDWAY

PLYMOUTH STADIUM, PENNYCROSS, PEVERELL.

3rd MEETING

APRIL 12TH **1932.** At 7-45 p.m.

Printed by R. T. RULE, 78 Cambridge Street, Plymouth.   Phone 209.

IMAGES *of Sport*

PLYMOUTH
SPEEDWAY

PAUL EUSTACE

TEMPUS

Front cover: Pete Lansdale rode for the Plymouth speedway team for six seasons and is the all-time highest scorer with 1,546 league points.

Back cover: On 15 May 1959 Belle Vue's Peter Craven established a new Pennycross track record of 70.6 seconds which has never been beaten.

Frontispiece: The cover of the programme used in Plymouth Speedway's first season in the National League in 1932 was coloured orange and black. The programme was printed locally by R.T. Rule of 78 Cambridge Street.

First published 2006

Tempus Publishing Limited
The Mill, Brimscombe Port,
Stroud, Gloucestershire, GL5 2QG
www.tempus-publishing.com

British Library Cataloguing in Publication Data.
A catalogue record for this book is available from the British Library.

ISBN 0 7524 4023 3

Typesetting and origination by Tempus Publishing Limited.
Printed in Great Britain.

Contents

Acknowledgements

No book relating the history of a speedway track can be complete without the photographs that help bring to life the images that exist in the minds of supporters. This book is no different and my grateful thanks go to the photographers whose work has been reproduced here – both those I have acknowledged and those who remain unknown.

My thanks go to the writers and editors of a host of books, magazines, articles, local newspapers, Plymouth Speedway programmes and brochures, that have provided me with information.

The closeness of the speedway fraternity is generated by a common interest in the sport that we love. This has been evident by the generosity shown to me while I have been putting together this book. My sincere appreciation goes to speedway friends Graham Haynes, Peter Jackson, the late Maurice Jones, Tony Lethbridge, John Somerville and, in particular, Len Read and John Walters, who have given me access to material and photographs without which this publication would not have been possible. I also wish to thank those others with whom I have discussed aspects of this project.

My final thanks are reserved, as always, for my lovely wife Jennie, whose unquestioning support is so appreciated.

The author at Beaulieu Motor Cycle World with 1950 Plymouth Devil Cecil Bailey, who is now in his eighty-eighth year. (Brian Thornton)

Introduction

My interest in speedway racing began in 1947 when I was first taken to Pennycross Stadium in Plymouth and to Southampton's Banister Court. At the time, both tracks were run by the same promoting company, Southern Speedways Limited, which was in charge at Plymouth for four years and Southampton for four and a half. At Pennycross I would sit at the first bend on a tarpaulin covering the greyhound track, with my back against the surrounding wall, together with hundreds of other young enthusiasts. My favourites in those days, apart from the Devils and the Saints, were top Division Three riders like Cyril Roger, Wally Green, Alan Hunt and Arthur Payne, who all became stars at the highest level of the sport in later years.

In pre-war times, Plymouth were members of the National League for three seasons and all the best riders visited Pennycross. Frank Arthur, Tom Farndon, Vic Huxley, Ron Johnson, Billy Lamont, Jack and Norman Parker, Tiger Stevenson and Colin Watson, to name just a few, thrilled the local supporters with their expertise on the track.

The dizzy heights of the First Division were not reached by the Plymouth team after the war but racing in the Second and Third Divisions was close and exciting to the committed fan. One looks back with nostalgia and happy memories and it is hoped that readers will share that feeling when they look at the photographs and read the supporting text.

2006 is the year when the people of the South West can look forward with hope and anticipation as a new track emerges in Plymouth. Gone for the time being is speedway in Exeter and Cornwall. The new track at Marsh Mills is ideally situated where the A38 Devon Expressway from Exeter meets the Parkway which leads to Cornwall. The promoter and organisers of the new Plymouth Devils are to be commended for relaunching speedway in the city for the first time in thirty-six years, and they are wished every success.

Meanwhile, through the pages of this book, the reader will be reminded of many of the men in leathers who graced the Pennycross track all those years ago.

Paul Eustace
March 2006

Pre-war Pennycross Stadium. Greyhound racing first took place at the stadium at Easter 1928, followed by speedway racing in June 1931. The track was flat and just over 400 yards in length. There was covered accommodation on both straights and the fourth bend, and the pits area was just in front of the totalisator. In the right foreground is the Cherry Tree public house which was opened on 1 April 1937. It was popular with post-war speedway fans and the licensee Mr Fred Titmuss, a former Plymouth Argyle footballer and England international, regularly donated a second-half trophy.

one

Twenty-two Seasons at Pennycross

The Cinders Come to Pennycross

With the arrival of dirt-track racing in England in 1928, and after the success of the meeting organised by Ilford Motor Club secretary Jack Hill-Bailey at High Beech on 19 February, tracks opened up all over the country. Many of them were laid in stadiums that were used for greyhound racing.

Pennycross Stadium in Plymouth was such a place. Greyhound racing had started there in 1928 and there was much discussion among local businessman about investing in and building a track that could accommodate the exciting new motor sport. Plymouth's near neighbours at Exeter had introduced speedway racing in 1929 at the County Ground Stadium and Plymothians were very keen to see it in their city. They had to wait until 1931 when a company called Western Speedway Limited, chaired by local motor car dealer Percy Fletcher, introduced the cinders to Pennycross Stadium. The man appointed to look after the track and manage the riders was Freddie Hore, who had raced at Exeter, White City (London) and Leicester Super.

There was no shortage of young men eager to try their luck on a speedway track, as motorcycling activities were already very popular in Devon and Cornwall. However, Fletcher and his fellow directors were shrewd enough to realise that, in order to capture and maintain the interest of the local population, established racers and not mere novices would be needed to form the basis of any side put together to represent the city of Plymouth. With this in mind, the company scoured the country to find the men they needed. Most of the other promoters were supportive of the new venture and were willing to release riders that they did not require for their own teams.

A nucleus of nine or ten riders, with some local novices, was assembled and practices took place on the new Pennycross track until gradually the team began to take shape. Bert Spencer, who had ridden for Exeter and Leicester Super, was appointed captain. He was joined by Australians Maurice Bradshaw, Bert Jones and later Paddy Dean, who had all ridden for West Ham, and Noel Johnson from Exeter. Completing the line-up was New Zealander Spencer Stratton (Sheffield and Nottingham), George Preston (Harringay) and another recruit from West Ham, Peter Slade.

The very first meeting at Pennycross, held on Saturday 13 June, was the first leg of the Devon Derby against county rivals Exeter. The Plymouth side triumphed 32-21 which pleased the home crowd of just over 6,000. Australians Bradshaw and Jones top scored with 7 points each, followed by skipper Spencer with 6, Slade and Stratton with 4 each, Preston 3 and Johnson 1.

Three days later, on Tuesday 16 June, Exeter had their revenge at the County Ground with a 33-20 victory to win the very first Devon Derby on aggregate. Noel Johnson gave a much improved performance for Plymouth, scoring 7 points from his three rides on his former track. Bradshaw and Slade scored 4 each, Spencer 3 and Jones 2 while Stratton failed to score. The two-leg Devon Derby competition became very popular with the Plymouth and Exeter supporters in the post-war years. Unfortunately, a month after the first one, County Speedways, the company running speedway at Exeter, went into liquidation so for much of the remaining pre-war years the only speedway seen in Devon was at Pennycross.

Tragedy Strikes on the Track

A number of challenge matches were held against teams from the Southern League. Although attendances fluctuated between 5,000 and 10,000, there was much interest in seeing the star riders from the established clubs. Narrow wins were achieved over Lea Bridge 26½-25½, Southampton 30-24 and West Ham 27-24, with a bigger win of 40-13 over a weak Exeter side.

Freddie Hore, the first track and team manager of Plymouth Speedway, was born in Exeter. A garage mechanic, he emigrated to Australia where he first started motorcycle racing. He came back to Britain in 1929, returned to his home town and rode at the County Ground for the Exeter team. Hore moved about in 1930 and raced at the vast Leicester Super track at Melton Road and also at London White City before taking up his position at Pennycross in 1931. He looked after the Tigers in their first league season in 1932 but relinquished the team manager's role the following year when it was taken over by Percy Fletcher.

Tragedy struck on 25 August when Plymouth's star Australian Noel Johnson crashed in the meeting against Coventry and died later in hospital. The fatal accident to the popular Johnson badly affected the other riders and subsequent results were not so good. There were defeats by Wimbledon 38-16, Stamford Bridge 35-18, High Beech 29-25, West Ham 33-21 and Crystal Palace 36-17, interspersed with a second victory over Lea Bridge 29-24 and a narrow defeat 27-26 at Leicester Super on 8 September, when skipper Spencer scored a maximum against his old team. The introductory season at Pennycross was deemed to be a success by Percy Fletcher and the other directors of Western Speedway Limited, and as a result the Plymouth team was accepted into the new National League for 1932.

The Tigers Enter the National League

The National League replaced the old Southern and Northern Leagues which had operated from 1929. Only Spencer, Slade, Jones and Bradshaw remained from the first season and the last three named mainly appeared in the second-half scratch races in 1932.

There was an influx of new riders at Pennycross as the promotion tried to build a match-winning side. Prominent newcomers were Bill Clibbett (Harringay and Wimbledon), Billy Ellmore (Leicester and Nottingham), Frank Goulden (Southampton and Clapton), Frank Pearce (High Beech) Jack Barber (Sheffield) together with Australians Stan Lupton and Eric Collins (Lea Bridge), Jack Jackson (Wembley), Clem Mitchell (Crystal Palace) and Ray Taylor (Southampton and Clapton).

During the first half of the season teams competed in the National Speedway Association Trophy and this was followed by the National Speedway League Championship. The Tigers, as Plymouth were known, wore orange and white race jackets and finished bottom in both competitions, winning just six of their thirty-four matches. They were also knocked out of the National Trophy in the first round by Clapton, 107-79 on aggregate. However, the statistics do not tell the whole story as throughout the season the national speedway press was full of compliments for the hard riding and wholehearted efforts of the Plymouth team. Early in the season, machine troubles and a large turnover of riders did not help, but when a more settled line-up was found things improved.

Frank Pearce led the team initially, in Spencer's absence, but unfortunately broke his arm badly in June. Spencer handed over the captaincy to Bill Clibbett that same month, and together with Eric Collins, Clibbett invariably topped the scorechart. Clibbett and Collins qualified for the 'Star' Championship final at Wembley on 22 September, but Collins was injured and replaced by Bert Spencer. Collins was very unlucky because such had been his form that he was selected for the Australian Test side but missed out through illness.

The 1933 National League table reflects that Plymouth made progress by finishing in ninth position, one place above wooden spoonists Nottingham. However, they had the same number of points as Coventry and Sheffield, the seventh and eighth placed teams. Eric Collins had returned to Australia but Bill Clibbett again skippered the side, which also included 1932 riders Bert Spencer, Frank Goulden and Jack Jackson. The new signings were Bill Stanley and Ted Bravery from Stamford Bridge, Reg Stanley from Lea Bridge and Australians John Glass (formerly Mick Murphy) of Wimbledon and Jack Sharp. Percy Fletcher replaced Freddie Hore as team manager.

Champions Belle Vue only lost five league matches out of thirty-six and one of them was at Pennycross where the Tigers won 34-29. The whole team scored solidly, with Bravery, Spencer, Stanley, Goulden and Sharp each winning a heat. Curiously, Plymouth won at Coventry 45-18 in May and then lost to the Midlanders by the same score at home in September. Although they beat Nottingham 64-62 at Pennycross on 20 June in the first round of the National Trophy, with both Goulden and Bravery scoring a splendid 16 points, the Tigers lost the return 81-42 despite fine performances by Clibbett and Sharp, who each scored 14 points. Plymouth went out of the competition on aggregate 143-106.

An unlucky day for the Tigers was 13 June when Bert Spencer fractured his leg in a first-heat collision with Keith Harvey at West Ham. He did not appear again in 1933 but an excellent late-season signing was German champion Sebastian Roth, who proved to be well up to National League standard. Among his scores was a 12-point maximum in the fine 35-27 victory over Wembley on 12 September. Plymouth's two representatives in the 'Star' Championship final at the Empire Stadium on 8 September were Jack Sharp and Frank Goulden. Sharp also rode in two Tests for Australia against England. The racing at Pennycross in 1933 was of a high standard and the local fans responded by turning out in numbers to support their team.

Plymouth Speedway had a difficult year in 1934, both on and off the track. Results were poor, with only eight league wins in thirty-two matches. As in the previous season, the team finished next to bottom in the table. Oddly, they again triumphed over eventual champions Belle Vue with a 31-22 win in September, when at the same meeting Max Grosskreutz smashed the Plymouth track record. More performances like that would have kept the supporters happy. Two old favourites resumed riding: Bert Spencer came back to the action after his accident in 1933 and Frank Pearce also reappeared at Pennycross after being out of racing for nearly two years. He had a memorable meeting at Wembley on 8 May when he broke the track record. The only significant newcomer was Phil 'Tiger' Hart until later in the season when Austrian Leopold Killmeyer made a good impression before getting injured.

In July Jack Sharp replaced an out-of-form Bill Clibbett as captain and was usually Plymouth's top scorer. He rode for Australia in all five Tests against England and he and Mick Murphy, who rode under his real name, John Glass, in 1933, represented Plymouth in the 'Star' Championship final at Wembley on 23 August.

Crowd support was well down and finances were tight. It was touch and go whether Plymouth would complete the season, but they did. Lea Bridge were given a walkover in round one of the National Trophy when the West Country side failed to ride there on 6 June after losing to the Londoners 57-49 at home on 22 May. Plymouth also failed to fulfil a league fixture at Belle Vue on 2 June and the Aces were awarded the match 36-0. Western Speedway Limited were not prepared to continue to sustain significant financial losses and so declared that they would not be running speedway at Pennycross in 1935.

Open Season at Pennycross

Speedway was not totally lost to the Plymouth public as Jack Colebach obtained an open licence and planned to put on a series of challenge matches in the new season to assess whether there was sufficient interest to justify the sport carrying on at Pennycross. Although Colebach retained the traditional orange and white colours, he decided that the riders he would book to race under the new promotional banner would be known as the 'Panthers'.

The first meeting was an individual event on 17 July, watched by a crowd of nearly 4,000. Last season's captain, Jack Sharp, opened up the proceedings by riding through the tapes which were in Plymouth's colours. The main competition was a scratch race for the Raven Trophy. It was won by Harringay's Australian Harry 'Tiger' Lewis in a time of 80.3 seconds. The runner-up was 1932 Plymouth rider Ray Taylor, now based at Wembley. New Cross junior Mike Erskine won the Flying Nine over three laps in 59.3 seconds and Taylor was again runner-up. The South African former Stamford Bridge and West Ham rider Keith Harvey won the Plymouth Distance Handicap in 83.3 seconds. The meeting was a great success and, if interest could be maintained, Colebach's effort to keep speedway going in Plymouth would be worthwhile.

The first match in which a Plymouth team competed was at the beginning of August against a team from the Hackney club and, although the Panthers lost, a good crowd returned on 11 August for a match against Southampton. The Saints were also out of league speedway at the time and their line-up consisted of riders from Charlie Knott's Harringay stable. The Panthers gained a resounding 42-30 victory and the hero and top scorer was the Australian pioneer rider Billy Lamont, who was on Wembley's books. He got a faultless maximum and thrilled the crowd with his exciting style. He was well supported by Hackney's New Zealander Jack Hobson with 10 points. Former Plymouth rider Bert Jones did best for the Hampshire side with 9 points.

Even more resounding was the Panthers' 40-13 win on 20 August over a very weak Cardiff team, three of whose selected riders failed to put in an appearance. Australian Jack Bibby scored a 9-point maximum, as did former Pennycross favourite Ted Bravery. This was a hollow victory and did not help the promoter to convince the locals that speedway was a sport worth watching. A further win over Eastbourne, who had Charlie Dugard and Phil Hart at the helm, was more encouraging for Colebach and he was beginning to formulate a side that he hoped to enter in league speedway in 1936.

The final match, against a team of London riders, ended in a defeat for the Panthers and the last meeting of the short season was the Plymouth Trophy on 10 September, won by Harringay's Bert Jones. Although the attendance for the final meeting was just under 3,000, Colebach felt the time was right to bring back league speedway to Pennycross.

Provincial League Speedway for the Panthers

A new Provincial League was formed in 1936 consisting of six teams, including the Panthers. Colebach managed to secure the services of many of the riders who had ridden for him in the open season but Harry Lewis, with whom he was so impressed, rode for Southampton, along with several of the Harringay-based riders.

Initially, Les Gregory skippered the side as he had in 1935, but later Australian Dick Wise took over the job. Wembley junior Les Bowden was the Panthers' top scorer, closely followed by Wise. Billy Lamont returned, was brilliant one day and poor the next but his racing electrified the crowd. Jack Bibby, Jack Hobson, Fred Tuck, Sam Marsland and Don Hemmingway all appeared in a largely settled team.

However, results were not good with only six wins in twenty-six matches in the league and the Provincial Trophy. As in 1935, the biggest win was against Cardiff but the Welsh side soon fell by the wayside and resigned from the league, so the result did not count. The Panthers finished bottom of the league table and fourth out of six in the trophy placings. Individually, the Plymouth riders did not shine. The Provincial League Riders' Championship was organised over five rounds and was won by the experienced George Greenwood of Nottingham with 59 points. Dick Wise finished well down the order with 29, Jack Hobson got 23 and Les Gregory 12.

Colebach is to be commended for running in 1936 but he could not produce the winning team that the fans craved. Once again there was to be no league speedway at Pennycross Stadium.

There was one meeting, however, held at Plymouth in the 1937 season. On 12 May an England side met an Australian team and in a closely fought encounter drew 27-27. There was local interest for the crowd of just under 5,000 with former Plymouth favourites Bill Clibbett, Ted Bravery, Billy Lamont and Jack Sharp taking part. In the second half, Billy Lamont won the Coronation Cup individual event. It was rumoured that a London company would be arranging more meetings but none were forthcoming, so speedway was lost to Pennycross for ten years.

The Devils Arrive at Pennycross

Speedway returned to Pennycross after the war on 24 April 1947, under the control of Southern Speedways Limited and promoter Jimmy Baxter, who had introduced league racing to speedway in 1929. The same organisation ran the sport at Southampton but the league positions of the Saints and the Devils, whose race jackets now featured a red devil on a yellow background, could not have been more contrasting.

Both sides had been entered in the new Third Division of the National League and for most of the season the Saints looked potential champions, eventually finishing third, 1 point behind champions Eastbourne and runners-up Cradley Heath. The Devils, on the other hand, propped up the rest of the league, finishing 9 points behind Wombwell. Many riders were given opportunities at Pennycross; most failed to make any impression. Mechanical problems were frequent which made life very difficult for beleaguered team manager Peter Slade, a pre-war Plymouth rider. Few matches were won, but a more settled side towards the end of the season offered hope for the future.

Cornishman Ivan Kessell, Stan Lanfear and Alex Gray were the riders best able to compete, with skipper Billy Newell and leg-trailer Charlie Challis producing the thrills and spills. One of the Devils' future stars, Len Read, was signed from Norwich in late August and soon became a big favourite of the fans. Despite the lack of success, crowds were loyal and consistent attendances of 10,000-plus were very encouraging for the management.

A far more competitive team was tracked in 1948 with Peter Robinson, Southampton's best rider in 1947, signed from Wembley after he had decided not to ride in Division One for health reasons. Captain Billy Newell won the John A. Chapman Trophy at the opening meeting of

Above left: When speedway resumed in Plymouth in 1947 it was run by Southern Speedways Limited with George 'Jimmy' Baxter as Director of Racing. He had promoted before the war at Glasgow, West Ham and Southampton and the company also ran speedway at Banister Court in the early post-war years.

Above right: One of Baxter's right-hand men was Freddie Frape, whose value to the promotion could not be overestimated. He undertook many of the backroom duties, including those of machine examiner, track manager and team manager. Frape continued to be involved at Pennycross with the various promoting companies up to the closure of the track in 1954.

the season in front of a 20,000 crowd but, after a loss of form, moved on to new side Rayleigh for £50 later in the season. Ted Gibson arrived from Tamworth and Australian Bonnie Waddell came from Newcastle via Exeter while Stan Lanfear travelled up the A38 to join the Falcons. Robinson and another ex-Saint, Pete Lansdale, together with Len Read, formed a strong heat-leader trio. Alex Gray was a solid performer and Ivan Kessell and Bonnie Waddell were usually effective second strings. Gibson did well but missed many matches with a broken ankle. Local rider Vic Gent showed an aptitude for away tracks and at the end of the season moved to Exeter, where he became a big star for several years. First-year novice Wally Matthews did as well as could be expected. The Devils benefited from the injured Wembley captain, Bill Kitchen, acting as tactical adviser for nearly six months of the season. Kitchen, who always spent his holidays in Devon and Cornwall, volunteered to help the Devils. Their progress could be gauged by their defeat of eventual champions Exeter at the County Ground at the end of August, with Len Read scoring a brilliant 11 points. That victory helped to make up for the big 65-31 defeat at Exeter on 24 May when sugar was found in the fuel tanks of Plymouth riders Pete Lansdale and Peter Robinson. A mid-table position was a big improvement on the previous season.

Even greater improvement was seen in season 1949. A new track surface of powdered brick dust replaced the decomposed Dartmoor granite which had been used in the two previous seasons and Freddie Frape was established as team manager. Lansdale, Read and Robinson showed brilliant form and they had good second-string support from first-year riders Alan Smith and George Wall and another newcomer from Southampton, Johnny Bradford. Track manager Gordon Parkins and Alex Gray had been transferred to Jimmy Baxter's new track at Liverpool and if Gray had stayed the Devils would have been serious title contenders. New signings New Zealander Bob Wigg and Geoff Woodger showed promise but 1948 riders Gibson, Waddell and Wally Matthews only lasted half the season. Ivan Kessell produced few good scores but was still a big favourite, and a creditable fifth place in the league was attained.

Promotion and Demotion

Plymouth were promoted to Division Two of the National League in 1950 and gave a very good account of themselves, topping the table until the middle of the season. Lansdale, Robinson, Read, Smith and Wall competed well at the higher level but new signing Cecil Bailey, who had scored heavily for the Devils' sister track at Southampton in the Second Division in 1949, was a disappointment. He returned to Banister Court in August and immediately looked a much better rider. Ivan Kessell retired from the track after struggling to find any real form and newcomers Dennis Hayles and Wally Mawdsley were given opportunities. The Devils faded towards the end of the season after Bradford and new signing Bill Thatcher suffered serious injuries. Former Exeter captain Bronco Slade was signed to fill the gap but his best years were behind him and he made no impact. The Devils did well to finish in mid-table.

When Plymouth Speedway resumed for the 1951 season it was not only in a lower grade, having been demoted to the Third Division for 'geographical reasons' after a very successful 1950 season in Division Two, it was also under completely new management. Control of the track at Pennycross Stadium had passed from Southern Speedways Limited to Plymouth Sports Stadium Limited, the owners of the circuit. Freddie Parr, the General Manager of the stadium, took over the promoter's reins from Jimmy Baxter and three favourites left Pennycross: Peter Robinson and Len Read went to Baxter's track at Liverpool and Lansdale joined Walthamstow. Both of these teams were in the Second Division. Former Exeter and Poole rider Sid Hazzard took over from Alan Briggs as team manager, while Freddie Frape continued as track manager.

More Tragedy on the Track

The new stars at Pennycross were captain George Wall, Alan Smith and Bill Thatcher. Alan Smith headed the Third Division averages and finished runner-up to Poole's Ken Middleditch in the Division Three Riders' Championship final at Cardiff. Smith and Wall were selected for the England 'C' and Young England sides. Johnny Bradford, local rider Brian Hitchcock and new signings Ron Barrett (Harringay), George Craig (Swindon) and Frank Wheeler (Poole) gave sound support. Dennis Hayles and Doug Fursey were the most promising of a number of poor-performing second strings and reserves and yet again a halfway position in the league was achieved. Tragedy struck in a junior scratch race on 3 May when thirty-six-year-old Dick Jenkins, making his first appearance on the Pennycross track, seemed to be in difficulty coming out of the second bend. Riding down the back straight at full throttle, he was unable to negotiate the bottom bends and literally rode up the fence and over the top. Jenkins was thrown on to the greyhound track and was fatally injured.

1952 saw Division Three become the Southern League and with the return of Pete Lansdale strengthening the side, the Devils led the table for much of the season. A poor finish after Lansdale's premature retirement in August meant the Devils were placed third, with George Wall and Alan Smith the top two riders in the Southern League averages. Skipper Wall scored maximums on two visits to champions Rayleigh, the only rider in the league to get full points at the Weir Stadium. He also won the Match Race Championship by defeating the holder,

Sid Hazzard, left, discussing the night's programme with Devils skipper George Wall and Bill Thatcher at a meeting in 1953. Bournemouth born Hazzard joined Plymouth as team manager and chief mechanic in 1951 and was very popular with both the riders and the fans. After starting on the grass he had a season racing at Exeter in 1947 and moved to Poole when they opened a year later. Hazzard took over as team manager at Wimborne Road in 1949 for two seasons before moving to Pennycross where he stayed until the beginning of 1954 when Don Weekes was appointed as team manager by the new promotion.

Rayleigh star Jack Unstead. John Deeley took over in June as team manager but resigned at the end of the season. Bill Thatcher always gave of his best, Hitchcock was an enigma with a mixed bag of performances, Bradford moved on to St Austell and Fursey and Wheeler were the best of the rest. Australian Ted Stevens, signed in June, looked to be a future heat leader but Roy Moreton, who had top scored for Wolverhampton in 1951 and was recruited to replace Pete Lansdale, could not match the former Devil's consistent double-figure scoring.

Pete Lansdale came out of retirement in 1953 and Len Read returned in May, which pleased the supporters, but a pre-season injury to skipper George Wall and, more tragically, the death of young Australian Ted Stevens after a crash at St Austell, seemed to knock the spirit out of the side. These blows, together with the use of too many reserves, resulted in a bottom placing. Sid Hazzard returned as team manager and on track Alan Smith was again the star of the team, with Lansdale and Bill Thatcher also performing well. The best support came from Stan Clark, Derek Timms and former Cardiff star, New Zealander Kevin Hayden. Well-known names Dick Howard and Johnny Sargeant were signed to boost the lower order without success. Both did better when they moved on to Exeter and St Austell respectively. Ironically, Sargeant top scored for the Gulls with 11 points when they beat the Devils 48-36 in a challenge match at the Cornish Stadium at the beginning of September.

National League Division Two and Closure

The mid-1950s were difficult times for speedway and in 1954 the Second Division and the Southern League amalgamated to form a National League Division Two consisting of fifteen teams. At Pennycross, a new consortium of R.C. Byng, R.W. Pritchard Jones and C.D. Gray took over, with Cyril Gray taking responsibility for promoting. Don Weekes, formerly associated with Exeter and Swindon, was appointed team manager and mechanic. Gray promised to strengthen the team to compete in the new league and with St Austell having closed he secured the services of their top two, Australians Jackie Gates and Harold Bull, together with New Zealander Kevin Bock. Gray tried to re-sign Johnny Sargeant but the rider chose to return to Exeter, where he had been a big favourite for many years. Youngsters Ken Holmes from Wimbledon and New Zealander Hec Mayhead from Wembley were added to the team. In May, Exeter's former captain Vic Gent returned to his home-town club. With Smith, Lansdale, Thatcher, Wall and a revitalised

Kevin Hayden, the team looked strong enough but it failed to perform. Bad weather and poor support did not help and the side's days were numbered. The Devils did not complete their Southern Shield fixtures and after only two league matches they withdrew from the league. The final meeting before the track closed was a World Championship qualifying round on 8 July. The meeting was run in a thick, misty drizzle which made the track treacherous and in which it was difficult for the riders to see. Southampton's Brian McKeown won the meeting with a 15-point maximum, with Swindon's Bob Roger second and Rayleigh's Peter Clark third. The Plymouth scorers were Smith 11, Lansdale 11, Mayhead 7, Thatcher 6, Gent 5 and Bull 2.

Seasons 1951-1954 had seen Alan Smith, George Wall and Bill Thatcher develop into reliable heat leaders and Pete Lansdale always gave good value. The major problem during these years was poor second strings and reserves. The track itself was good, with very little home advantage, so visiting sides generally performed well. The 'derbys' against local rivals Exeter and St Austell were always hard fought and exciting. Despite the lack of any real league success, regular supporters will have many happy memories of their visits to Pennycross over these four seasons. Plymouth's best riders soon found new homes: Alan Smith signed for Southampton but after Control Board intervention – and much to Saints promoter Charlie Knott's disgust – he went to First Division West Ham; Pete Lansdale and George Wall went to Rayleigh, Hec Mayhead to Birmingham and Bill Thatcher moved to Oxford, where he linked up again with former Plymouth captain Peter Robinson.

Speedway Again at Pennycross

Five years went by, during which time there was much local chat, gossip and speculation about speedway returning to Pennycross Stadium. Supporters were pleased when they learned that Western Promotions, with Trevor Redmond and Eric Netcott, planned to run some meetings in 1959. In effect there were five, and some of the best riders of the day appeared, like Ove Fundin, Barry Briggs, Split Waterman, Ken McKinlay, Ronnie Moore, Geoff Mardon and Peter Craven. Former Plymouth favourites Alan Smith and Pete Lansdale also wore the Devils' race jacket again.

The first meeting on Good Friday 27 March between Plymouth and the Midlands attracted an attendance of over 10,000. Split Waterman captained the Devils and a close match resulted in a 49-47 win for the Midlands in showery conditions. Leading scorers for the home team were Ray Cresp, with a 15-point maximum, Lansdale and Waterman with 10 each and Alan Smith with 6. Jack Biggs top scored for the visitors with 13 points.

Over 5,000 returned for the Best Pairs meeting held on Thursday 23 April, which was won by Wimbledon. Ronnie Moore scored a five-ride maximum and Bob Andrews added another 4 points. The Plymouth pairings of Neil Street (11) and Alan Smith (5½) and George White (11) and Pete Lansdale (1) finished third and fifth respectively. Poole's Ray Cresp broke the track record with a time of 71.4 seconds in the first race of the evening.

Peter Craven led Plymouth to victory over Oxford by 54-42 on Friday 15 May with a sparkling 15-point maximum and also established a new track record of 70.6 seconds. Neil Street 12, George White 11, Mike Broadbanks 10 and Alan Smith and Jimmy Squibb 3 completed the Devils' scoring with Arne Pander notching 11 for the Cheetahs.

The contest on Friday 7 July between a Combined Stars side and the Swedish Lions, which ended in a 48-48 draw, was the best meeting of the short season. Well presented by Trevor Redmond, the racing between Geoff Mardon, Ken McKinlay and Swedish stars Ove Fundin and Rune Sormander was breathtaking and the West Country crowd was absolutely enthralled. Fundin and Sormander scored 15 points apiece and Mardon and McKinlay each got 10.

The final meeting was on Thursday 3 September with Ken McKinlay's Lions defeating Barry Briggs' Overseas Stars 38-34, with McKinlay and Briggs top scoring for their respective teams.

Crowds were good enough in 1959 to encourage Eric Salmon, who was part of the Bristol promotion, to plan a Western Cup competition in 1960 between Plymouth, Exeter, Bristol and St Austell. In the event, only one match was held at Pennycross, with Plymouth, represented by Poole, drawing 36-36 with Bristol in front of a 4,000 crowd on Thursday 8 September. Ross Gilbertson and Tony Lewis each got 10 for Plymouth and Johnny Hole and Cliff Cox scored 9 each for the Bulldogs. In the second half Francis Cann was lucky to get away with only concussion after demolishing part of the safety fence on the second bend.

A week later, the second and final meeting was a qualifying round of the Provincial League Riders' Championship, won with a 15-point maximum by Rayleigh's Eric Hockaday, who the following year would captain the Exeter Falcons.

Bulldogs and Devils in the Provincial League

Despite finishing third in the newly formed Provincial League in 1960, Bristol closed as Knowle Stadium was to be redeveloped, so the promotion moved their operation to Pennycross, unfortunately without the two star riders Trevor Redmond and Johnny Hole. Plymouth appeared to lack top-end strength and some supporters found it difficult to follow the Bulldogs rather than the Devils, but a very successful season ensued. This success was thanks to Eric Salmon managing to acquire Australian Jack Scott on loan from Southampton, where he had ridden for two seasons, Maury Mattingley moving from National League Coventry and Bristol-born Cliff Cox emerging as a strong captain and heat leader. Good support from Ron Bagley and Chris Julian meant the Bulldogs were runners-up to champions Poole. The exciting and spectacular Chris Blewett suffered very serious facial injuries after hitting the fence at Wolverhampton in July.

Jack Scott had an outstanding season and he was undoubtedly the best rider in the Provincial League. In his black and yellow sweater, he broke track records all over the country, appearing in the British Final of the World Championship at Wembley and riding for Great Britain against Sweden. Southampton constantly tried to get Scott back to Banister Court, but the Speedway Control Board would not allow it. Mattingley was brilliant, emerging top of the Provincial League World Championship qualifiers with a 15-point maximum at Poole and 14 points at Stoke. A week after his win at Poole, he scored another 15-point maximum on the same track for the Provincial League All Stars against the Pirates. He and Scott were joint top qualifiers in the Provincial League Riders' Championship, Mattingley winning at Edinburgh (14 points) and on his home track with 15. Scott was victorious at Newcastle with 15 and second to Mattingley with 14 at Pennycross. In the Provincial League Riders' Championship Final at Harringay on 16 September, Mattingley finished third behind Reg Reeves and Trevor Redmond and Scott was fourth. These achievements completed a very satisfactory first season back in league competition for Plymouth Speedway.

The Bulldogs were a stronger side than fierce rivals Exeter, which pleased local supporters, but it was strange to see Pete Lansdale in a Falcons' race jacket riding for the County Ground team, which he also co-promoted.

Changes were wholesale for the 1962 season. Supporters were thrilled to see the reappearance of the Devils' name and colours under new promoter Bernard Curtiss. Ron Bagley was lost to Sheffield and Jack Scott did not return from Australia, although if he had he would certainly have ridden for parent club Southampton in the National League.

Promoter Curtiss pulled off a masterstroke by signing Jimmy Squibb from National League Ipswich, and he more than adequately replaced Scott. He brought the Silver Sash Match Race title to Plymouth by defeating holder Ivor Brown of Cradley Heath in July. Squibb, Maury Mattingley and skipper Cliff Cox formed a very strong heat-leader trio and Chris Julian and Chris Blewett were nearly at that level, particularly at home. Blewett's forfeiting of his own maximum to memorably escort George Summers to a heat-twelve win against Leicester on 5 July was team riding at its best. Two points behind at the time, it was this 5-1 that clinched victory for the Devils. A glamour signing was made in former England captain Bert Roger, who was persuaded to come out of retirement to ride for the new Devils. He had captained Exeter to the 1948 Division Three championship before becoming a Test star with New Cross and West Ham. Squibb and Cox reached the final of the Provincial League Riders' Championship at Belle Vue on 22 September but had a disappointing evening.

The season promised much but things went wrong. Team manager Len Glover was summarily dismissed by Curtiss on 21 June and later Cy Melville took over that duty. Mattingley had long spells on the injured list and Roger retired in mid-season. Twice he scored maximums, so the ability was still there, but his heart didn't seem to be in it. The Devils' old problem of weak reserves meant only sixth position in the league was reached. Crowd support tailed off alarmingly and it was no surprise when Curtiss said he would not be running speedway at Pennycross in 1963. Former Rayleigh, Ipswich and Walthamstow rider Alby Smith, who had appeared for the Devils in 1962, applied for an open licence but was turned down by the Control Board, so there was to be no more speedway at Pennycross until 1968.

A New Era at Plymouth Speedway

Former Devils' hero of the 1940s and '50s Pete Lansdale returned to Pennycross Stadium in 1968 as promoter with Speedway Enterprises Limited and produced a very successful and entertaining side. They won all their home matches and had two of the biggest stars in the division in captain Mike Cake and Australian Chris Bass. Individually, Cake won the Guards Trophy at Plymouth on 2 August, a meeting in which new 2006 promoter Mike Bowden took part, and also the Bromley Bowl on 3 October. He was the top qualifier for the Division Two Riders' Championship final at Hackney on 27 September, but finished a disappointing seventh with 10 points. Fellow Devil Phil Woodcock scored 5. Chris Bass won the Cavalcade of Speed meeting at Pennycross on 2 September. Outstanding support was provided by Woodcock and seventeen-year-old Tony George, who won a plaque for being the most improved rider in his first season. With other regulars New Zealander Dave Whitaker, Frank Payne and Chris Roynon, the Devils had a settled line-up for most of the season.

The tarmac surface which had been used for stock-car racing was covered with silver sand and Lansdale and Bill Cake shared the team manager duties. Lansdale could not control the weather, however, and several meetings were rained off, which affected the enthusiasm of the supporters. The race night was changed from Friday to Thursday and back again, but still attendances were sparse, despite a fourth place in the league. Cake, Bass, Woodcock and George were owned by First Division Exeter, and it was clear that they would not be available to the Devils in 1969.

Pete Lansdale decided to sever his connections with Pennycross and Fred Osborn, the stadium manager, took over the promotion for the new season. Fifty-six-year-old former England star George Newton, who worked in a Cornish garage, was appointed team manager and coach. Osborn wanted to build up his own side, with no loaned riders, and finding new heat leaders was a priority. Dave Whitaker stepped up to take over the captaincy, Chris Roynon came back and improved, but the top two were Colin Sanders, a twenty-one-year-old unknown from Poole, and Bob Coles, who had had a handful of outings in 1968.

Sanders was a revelation, particularly at Pennycross, and it was mainly thanks to him that the majority of home matches were won. He qualified for the Division Two Riders' Championship Final at Hackney on 26 September but his lack of experience meant he only managed 5 points. Away from home the Devils had no success and were not helped by Whitaker, Ian Gills and Frank Payne suffering injuries which kept them out of the team for periods. Plymouth finished fifteenth in a sixteen-team league and the fact that they completed the season was an achievement in itself as they fielded a team that was weak from the start. Interest was raised when former captain Cliff Cox was persuaded to attempt a comeback but it didn't work. Inadequate machinery and track rustiness proved too much for the popular Bristolian. In the final home meeting of the season on 3 October, Bob Coles showed how much progress he had made with an unbeaten six rides to win the Bromley Bowl.

Speedway's Last Year at Pennycross

The 1970 season was to be the last year for speedway at Pennycross. Plymouth City Council had bought the stadium for £41,000 in 1962 and the original intention was to provide a new site for Sutton High School, a local grammar school situated in a poor position in the city centre. This never happened, however, and the stadium was allowed to deteriorate. Pennycross was in an ideal position for a sports stadium and, in hindsight, it would surely have been worth maintaining and improving it.

Support for speedway in 1969 had been poor and after much deliberation Fred Osborn had sold the league licence to Peterborough during the winter and decided to run an open season of challenge matches. He wanted time to build a team to compete again in league speedway, albeit in a different location. The tarmac track surface was dug up and replaced with blue shale, which it was hoped would lead to more competitive racing.

Plymouth opened their season on Good Friday 27 March before a crowd of over 2,000 who saw the Devils narrowly beaten 41-37 by Eastbourne. Poole and Reading guest Mike Vernam scorched to a 15-point maximum and Bob Coles contributed 10. On 10 April the Devils hammered Romford 53-24 with guest Mike Vernam getting 11 points and Bob Coles and Chris Roynon scoring 10 apiece. After these two meetings, Osborn was refused permission by the council to use the stadium for speedway and they leased it to local club owner John Weight. Weight ran a football team at the stadium called Plymouth City which included several former Plymouth Argyle players. He also wanted to re-introduce greyhound racing, which he said would not be compatible with speedway, although in the past both sports had lived happily together at the stadium.

Fred Osborn was nothing if not determined but negotiations with Weight had no success initially. Eventually agreement was reached for Osborn to continue promoting while Weight would look after the finance. Speedway restarted on 25 May with a big 51-27 win over Peterborough. Bob Coles top scored with 11 points and Colin Sanders was next with 10. Osborn had great difficulty in attracting riders to Plymouth because of the travelling distance, but given the circumstances he managed to put together an attractive side. It consisted of a fast-developing Bob Coles, Colin Sanders, Chris Roynon, John Hammond and a young discovery from Axminster, Clark Facey. Together with some experienced guest riders, the Devils won seven of their ten challenge matches.

There were victories over Swindon Juniors 46-32, Romford 43-34, Rayleigh 45-33, Crewe 46-32 and Newport Colts 53-24. The Devils were narrowly defeated by Reading 40-38 and again by Eastbourne, this time 43-35. Bob Coles (96), Colin Sanders (64) and Clark Facey (55) were the season's leading scorers and newcomers Dave O'Connor and Danny Dennis showed promise.

Unfortunately, the poor crowds of 1969 became even worse in 1970 and Osborn had to admit defeat. The track finally closed after the traditional Bromley Bowl meeting on 17 July, won by Eastbourne's Mac Woolford after a run-off with Colin Sanders, both having finished with 14 points. Historically, speedway supporters do not like meaningless challenge matches and this, together with the poor facilities, meant that the local enthusiasts stayed away. In 1972 the stadium was demolished and the site became a trading development so that was the end of speedway at Pennycross... but not, it would appear, the end of speedway in Plymouth.

A new track has been built at the St Boniface Arena, just off the A38 Devon Expressway at Marsh Mills, and the Plymouth Devils race again in 2006. Under the promotion of Mike Bowden, the team will compete in the Conference League. There is tremendous interest in the city and the surrounding areas of Devon and Cornwall in the new venture and it is wished every success.

two

The Pre-War Struggle 1931-1937

Pennycross favourite number one: Bert Spencer. Spencer was born in London in 1908, moving to Australia when he was three years old. He returned to England in 1928, linking up with Exeter in 1929 before moving to Leicester Super the following year. Spencer was made captain of Plymouth in 1931 and he stayed at Pennycross for four seasons, riding in the 'Star' Championship final at Wembley in 1932. His leg-trailing style was best suited to the bigger tracks. Although Spencer later had spells at Bristol and Wimbledon, his most successful period was at Pennycross, and also at Norwich where he rode both before and after the war. (*Speedway News*)

Opposite below: Twenty-six-year-old New Zealander Spencer Stratton came to England in 1928 after considerable success on the big tracks in Australia. Mainly based in the North and Midlands, he rode for Sheffield in 1929 and Nottingham a year later before moving to Pennycross for Plymouth's first season.

Above: Plymouth team, 1931. From left to right: Bert Spencer (captain), Bert Jones, Noel Johnson, –?–, Maurice Bradshaw, Peter Slade, Paddy Dean.

Above left: Australian Noel Johnson rode at Harringay before captaining Exeter in 1929. He joined Plymouth in 1931 and the fans loved him. There was great sadness when Johnson crashed at Pennycross on 25 August and died later from his injuries.

Above right: Paddy Dean came to England with a big reputation. His hair-raising style thrilled the crowds but he did not enjoy the success at Plymouth in 1931 that he had in Australia.

The Stamford Bridge team heavily defeated Plymouth 35-18 at Pennycross on 15 September 1931 in front of a 10,000 crowd. From left to right: Dick Smythe, Dick Wise, Frank Arthur (captain), Mr R. Cory (team manager), Wal Phillips, Gus Kuhn, Keith Harvey, Bill Stanley, Arthur Warwick. (*Speedway News*)

Twenty-one-year-old Midlander Tom Farndon was one of the greatest ever English riders. Riding for Crystal Palace in the last meeting of the 1931 season he established a new Pennycross track record of 79.2 seconds. He also won the Golden Helmet final in the second half.

London Cup winners Crystal Palace brought the 1931 Plymouth season to a close with an emphatic 36–17 victory over the West Country side. From left to right, back row: Jim Cowie, Bill Pitcher, Nobby Key, Triss Sharp, Ron Johnson, Tom Farndon. Front row: Alf Sawford, Roger Frogley (captain), Harry Shepherd, Joe Francis. (*Speedway News*)

Above: The 1932 Plymouth team which lost their second home match of the season 36–15 to 1931 league champions Wembley on 19 April. From left to right: Bert Jones, Bill Clibbett, Freddie Hore (team manager), Billy Ellmore, Frank Pearce (captain), Jack Barber, Jimmy Ewing, Stan Lupton.

Below: Australian Stan Lupton joined Plymouth from Lea Bridge in 1932. He scored two heat wins in the match against Wembley, including a brilliant defeat of England international Ginger Lees.

Above left: Australian Ray Taylor signed for Plymouth in July 1932 after riding for Southampton and Clapton. The Pennycross track suited him but he had more success at home in Australia. He later rode at Wembley and Wimbledon. (Wright Wood archive, courtesy of John Somerville)

Above right: London–born Frank Pearce excelled on the grass track at the Brisbane Exhibition Grounds. He came to England in 1928 and rode for High Beech in 1931. Pearce did well at Plymouth in 1932 but broke his arm in June against Coventry. He resumed his Pennycross career in 1934 and rode for Australia in 1934, 1935 and 1936.

Billy Ellmore was the second highest scorer at Leicester Stadium in 1929 and captained Nottingham for two years before suffering terrible injuries in a track crash. He attempted a comeback at Plymouth in 1932 but retired after just eight matches for the Tigers.

Above left: Jack Barber had three seasons at Sheffield before joining Plymouth in 1932. He rode in fourteen matches before losing his team place halfway through the season.

Above right: Australian Jack Jackson rode for Wembley from 1929 to 1931 but looked a much improved rider at Pennycross in 1932. He moved back to London, to Crystal Palace, early in the next season.

The Plymouth team which lost 35–19 on 23 April 1932 away at Crystal Palace. From left to right: Bill Clibbett, Billy Ellmore, Jack Barber, Tommy MacDonald, Stan Lupton, Bert Spencer (captain), Frank Pearce. Although defeated, the Plymouth team received great credit in the speedway press for their brave fight. (*Speedway News*)

Pennycross favourite number two: Bill Clibbett. Bristol-born Clibbett came to Pennycross after experience at open tracks Exeter and Portsmouth, and then Harringay and Wimbledon in 1931. He had a very successful three seasons with the Tigers, representing them at the 1932 'Star' Championship final at Wembley. Clibbett took over as captain from Bert Spencer in June 1932 but after a temporary loss of form was replaced by Jack Sharp halfway through 1934. The following year he moved to Hackney for three seasons before ending his career at Knowle Stadium in his home town. (*Speedway News*)

Queenslander Eric Collins began his career at Davies Park, Brisbane in 1928. He joined Harringay in 1931, also appearing for Lea Bridge. Collins started late at Pennycross in 1932 as he was recovering from losing a toe. He recovered well enough to suggest he would have topped the scorechart if he had not missed so many matches. He scored several maximums and was a match for the best riders in the league. Qualifying for the 'Star' Championship final, he was unlucky to miss it through injury. He was also selected for Australia but unable to ride because of illness. He was later attached to Wimbledon and Bristol. (*Speedway News*)

Collins looking very relaxed before his next race. (*Speedway News*)

One of the greatest pre-war riders, twenty-six-year-old Vic Huxley from Brisbane. He was the most outstanding rider to visit Pennycross Stadium in 1932. He scored a maximum 9 points for the Kangaroos in their 33-15 challenge match victory over the home team on 14 June and was then unbeaten for a London Select side that defeated the Tigers 32-22 in August. Huxley had yet another unbeaten meeting on 20 September when the Dons overcame Plymouth 29-22 in a league match. He also won all his second-half races. (*Speedway News*)

The Wimbledon captain, Vic Huxley, leads his Plymouth counterpart, Bill Clibbett, to win heat one of the league clash in September in a time of 78.3 seconds.

Plymouth team, 1932. From left to right: Bert Spencer, Frank Goulden, Jack Jackson, Frank Pearce (on machine), Bill Clibbett (captain), Clem Mitchell, Eric Collins.

Above left: Clem Mitchell came to Pennycross in 1932 after a season at Crystal Palace. He was far more successful in Australia and several times was at the top end of the scorecharts for his country. (*Speedway News*)

Above right: Bristolian Ted Bravery joined Plymouth in 1933 for two seasons. Previously he had ridden for Exeter and Stamford Bridge. He later rode for seven teams in the pre-war era before settling at Norwich in 1947. (Stenner's)

The man with two names: John Glass was christened Mick Murphy by Johnnie Hoskins in Australia in 1927 because he thought he looked Irish. He continued to be known as Murphy at Stamford Bridge in 1931 and at Wimbledon the next season. After riding on the Continent he arrived at Plymouth in 1933 and used his real name of John Glass. While racing at Sydney in the winter he met up again with Hoskins, who insisted that he revert to being known as Mick Murphy. Therefore, it was Mick Murphy who resumed at Plymouth in 1934 and rode in the 'Star' Championship final. John Glass was not Irish, nor even Australian. He was born in Fifeshire, Scotland on 20 March 1910. (*Speedway News*)

Above left: Reg Stanley joined the Tigers from Lea Bridge in July 1933 and although he had a regular place in the side was not a big scorer.

Above right: Twenty-three-year-old Frank Goulden signed for Plymouth halfway through the 1932 season after home town club Southampton had moved to Clapton. He had a good 1933 and rode in the 'Star' Championship final at the Empire Stadium. (*Speedway News*)

Midlander Bill Stanley rode for Coventry with the Parker brothers and Tom Farndon. He was at Stamford Bridge in 1931 and 1932 before joining Plymouth the following year. Stanley had two successful seasons at Pennycross.

Pennycross favourite number three: Jack Sharp. Australian Sharp must rank as one of Plymouth's best pre-war riders, alongside Bill Clibbett and Eric Collins. He made an immediate impact and had two outstanding seasons in 1933 and 1934. Sharp was one of the Tigers' representatives at the 'Star' Championship final in both of his years at Pennycross and also was selected to ride for his country in the Test matches against England. When the Tigers left the league in 1935 he went to Wimbledon, where he got injured after a few matches. However, he returned to Plough Lane for another two seasons before retiring and returning to Australia.

One of the greatest ever speedway riders, Ron Johnson, won the Plymouth Championship on 17 July 1934 with a 15-point maximum in a very strong field. Local fans judged his performance that day to be the most outstanding at Pennycross in the 1934 season. (*Speedway News*)

Above left: Phil 'Tiger' Hart was born in Balham, South London, but spent his formative years in Australia. Returning to England in 1930, he spent time at Portsmouth, Eastbourne and High Beech before having a good 1934 season at Pennycross. (*Speedway News*)

Above right: Former Plymouth rider Bert Jones returned to Pennycross twice in 1935. He top scored for Southampton with 9 points on 11 August and won the Plymouth Trophy with 10 points on 10 September. (Wright Wood archive, courtesy of John Somerville)

Above left: The 1936 programme was red and white in colour and printed by Austin C. Clark of Devonport.

Above right: Billy Lamont was from New South Wales and rode for London sides Wimbledon, Clapton and Wembley before coming to Pennycross in 1935. He stayed with the Panthers for their return to league racing the following year. (*Speedway News*)

Billy Lamont was known as 'Cyclone' and was spectacular to the point of recklessness. He was popular with the local fans, who held their breath when he was on the track. (Stenner's)

Plymouth team, 1936. Top, clockwise from the right: Sam Marsland, Jack Hobson, Les Bowden, Jack Bibby, Dick Wise (captain in centre). From left to right, bottom row: Fred Tuck, Les Gregory, Billy Lamont.

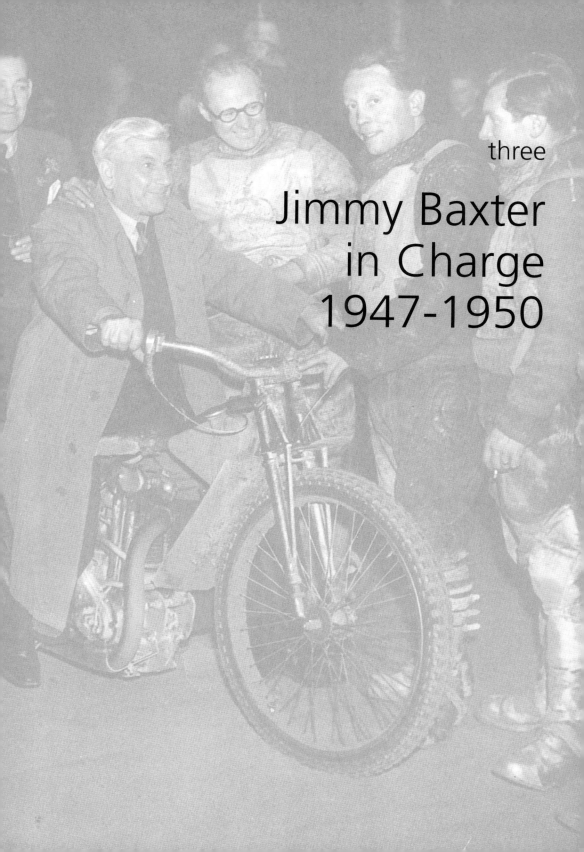

three

Jimmy Baxter
in Charge
1947-1950

Southern Speedways Ltd.

Directors—P. Bantock, E. Austin, J. Baxter, G. Parkins.

PRESENT

Programme of the

FIRST SPEEDWAY MEETING

—— SEASON 1947 ——

OFFICIALS

Direction of Speedway Racing—Jimmy Baxter
A.C.U. Steward—George R. Allen
A.C.U. Judge and Timekeeper
Clerk of the Course—Gordon Parkins
Announcer—Capt. Dakyns
Auto Cycle Union Track Licence No. (Provisional)

OPENING CEREMONY by THE LORD MAYOR OF PLYMOUTH
Councillor W. Harry Taylor
GRAND PARADE of Riders, Officials, St. John's Ambulance Brigade

PROGRAMME

THE LORD MAYOR'S TROPHY COMPETITION

This event will be run in a series of 20 races. The result will be decided on a score of points. Each Rider taking part will ride five times. In the event of a tie for highest points, the two Riders concerned will take part in a special "Match Race" over a distance of Three Laps. The winner of this event will be declared the winner of the Trophy.

POINTS. Heat winners : 3 Points ; 2nd, 2 Points ; 3rd, 1 Point.

TONIGHT'S RIDERS' INDIVIDUAL SCORE CHART

NAME	1	2	3	4	5	To.	NAME	1	2	3	4	5	To.
George Bason	3	3	3	3	3	15	Bill Deegan	2	2	1	ET	0	5
Bill Newell	2	1	2	3	3	11	Len Covell	1	2	0	1	1	5
John Scott	0	3	1	1	2	7	Alf Boyce	0	0	0	1	0	1
Ron Lemon	1	1	NS	NS	ET	2	Vic Collins	2	NS	2	2	3	9
Peter Robinson	3	3	2	3	2	13	Broncho Slade	3	NS	2	3	3	11
Vic Bernard	0	1	1	0	1	3	Ken Slee	1	NS	1	1	1	4
Edward Tyler	1	NS	0	0	0	1	Ivan Kessell	0	3	3	2	2	10
Jim Cashmore	2	2	F	0	2	6	A. L. Simpson	0					0
Matthew Hall	3	2	2	2	1	10	Dick Tamblin (Res.)	3	3				6
							Jim Squibb (Res.)	1					1

Above left: The attractive programme for the first meeting on Thursday 24 April 1947 was coloured red, yellow, black and white and printed by Clarke, Doble and Brendon Limited, Plymouth.

Above right: The scorechart for the Lord Mayor's Trophy competition.

The Lord Mayor of Plymouth, Mr W. Harry Taylor, opened the first speedway meeting at Pennycross Stadium since 1937 in front of a crowd of 9,000. He shakes hands with local rider Ken Slee while Ivan Kessell shares a joke with them. (*Western Morning News*)

Above left: Southampton's George Bason won the trophy at the opening meeting on 24 April 1947 with a 15-point maximum. (Southern Photographic Service)

Above right: Two points behind Bason was fellow Saint Peter Robinson, who was runner-up. (E.G. Patience)

The highest scoring Plymouth rider was Billy Newell, who shared third place with Exeter's captain Bronco Slade, both finishing with 11 points.

Cornish grass-track expert Ivan Kessell looks ready for the new season on the cinders.

Kessell practising hard on the Pennycross circuit. (Norman Studios)

Above left and right: Bristol born Stan Lanfear won the Southern Centre Championship and the Wessex Centre Championship on the grass before being signed by Wembley. He never rode for the Lions and was loaned to Plymouth where he was second highest scorer in the 1947 season. (E.G. Patience)

The Plymouth team which lost their first home league match of the 1947 season 43–41 against Tamworth on 15 May. From left to right: Vic Bernard, Bill Deegan, Ivan Kessell, Jim Cashmore, Billy Newell (captain), Len Covell, Des Tamblin, Stan Lanfear. Lanfear top scored with 11 points and Vic Bernard was patched up from his crash at Tamworth the previous night.

Belle Vue captain and England international Jack Parker presenting awards of electric clocks to Plymouth's Stan Lanfear and Ivan Kessell. They were runners-up to Southampton's George Bason and Peter Robinson in the Best Pairs competition at Exeter on 30 June 1947.

Above: Leg-trailer Charlie Challis rode at Birmingham and Crystal Palace before the war and joined Plymouth from Norwich in June 1947. He had several double-figure scores in his first season at Pennycross but lost his place in the side halfway through 1948. Challis moved to non-league Leicester as captain, together with Plymouth teammates Harold Sharp and George Argrave.

Opposite below: The Devils on their lap of honour after their big 54-29 win over Wombwell on 7 August 1947. From left to right: Harold Sharp with Charlie Challis riding pillion, Billy Newell with mascot Ronnie Partridge, Vic Gent, Stan Lanfear, Alex Gray and Ivan Kessell, who top scored with 11 points. (*Western Morning News*)

Above: The Plymouth team beaten 50-30 at Cradley Heath on 26 July 1947. From left to right: Harold Sharp, Vic Gent, George Argrave (kneeling), Ivan Kessell, Billy Newell (captain), Doug Bell, Gordon Parkins (team manager, kneeling), Charlie Challis, Alex Gray.

Above: Thirty-one-year-old Londoner Alex Gray makes it look easy as he takes a corner at Pennycross Stadium in 1947. (Norman Studios)

Below: Plymouth's Ivan Kessell leads three Cradley Heath riders at Dudley Wood Stadium.

Right: Twenty-seven-year-old Plymothian Vic Gent had some track experience in Germany during the war. Unreliable machinery hampered his early progress at Pennycross.

Below: The Plymouth team which defeated Exeter 47–36 in the Devon Derby in the last meeting of the season on 23 October 1947. From left to right, back row: Gordon Parkins (track manager), Ivan Kessell, Harold Sharp, Charlie Challis, Billy Newell (captain), Alex Gray, Peter Slade (team manager). Front row: Stan Lanfear, Len Read, Vic Gent. Alex Gray and Charlie Challis top scored with 9 points each. (*Western Morning News*)

Pennycross favourite number four: Ivan Kessell. Kessell was born in Cornwall and established a big reputation as an accomplished grass-track exponent. He had a few second-half rides at Banister Court before the war when working at Mike Erskine's motor engineering company. Kessell was top scorer for the Devils in his first season at Pennycross in 1947 and was very popular with the local supporters. He held his place in the side for two more seasons and retired from the track in 1950.

Pete Lansdale was the Devils' big signing from Southampton for the 1948 season. Here he leads Stan Hodson of Exeter. (Norman Studios)

Plymouth team, 1948. From left to right, back row: Jimmy Baxter (promoter), Roy Uden, Doug Bell, Harold Sharp, Ted Gibson, Bill Weston, Alex Gray, Gordon Parkins (track manager). Middle row: Pete Lansdale, Ken Slee, Billy Newell (captain), Ivan Kessell. Front row: Vic Gent, Len Read, Phil Day. (Stan Jay)

Plymouth's skipper Billy Newell taking the lead from Exeter's John Myson in the John A. Chapman Trophy competition on Good Friday 26 March 1948 at Pennycross Stadium, in front of a 20,000 crowd. Newell eventually won the trophy with 14 points, 2 more than runner-up Myson. (Norman Studios)

In the same meeting, George Bason (Southampton) leads Plymouth's Ivan Kessell, Alex Gray and Charlie Challis on the first bend. Bason and Challis each finished with 10 points, Gray 8 and Kessell 5. (Norman Studios)

Former Southampton star Peter Robinson arrived at Pennycross from Wembley in May and added considerable strength to the Devils' line-up. (Norman Studios)

Robinson taking a corner in his smooth and polished style. (Norman Studios)

Left: Bill Kitchen started his speedway career with Belle Vue in 1933 and within weeks of his debut was appearing for England at Hyde Road. He stayed with the Manchester side until the war. In 1946 the pooling system took him to the Empire Stadium and he was immediately made captain. On 13 April 1948 Kitchen received severe arm injuries at West Ham. Wembley's misfortune was Plymouth's gain for he agreed to act as tactical adviser to the Devils. They had the benefit of his experience until he returned to the track in August, continuing to lead Wembley with all his old craft and team-riding ability. (Norman Studios)

Below left: Plymouth's new signing Ted Gibson scored 128 league points for Tamworth in 1947 but injury curtailed his effectiveness at Pennycross. (Norman Studios)

Above right: Twenty-one-year-old Bristol-born Wally Matthews was a raw novice at the start of 1948 but held a regular place in the team in the second half of the season. (Norman Studios)

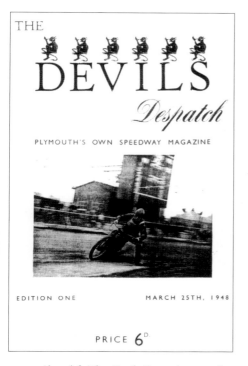

Above left: The *Devils Despatch* was a glossy magazine published fortnightly in 1948 and 1949. It was edited by Gordon Parkins and printed by Clarke, Doble and Brendon Limited.

Above right: On 8 April 1948 it was suggested in the magazine that the Devils adopt the Dick Barton signature tune. However, it was not possible to do so for copyright reasons.

Plymouth's Alex Gray having a tussle with Exeter's Don Hardy and Hugh Geddes in the Anniversary Cup at Pennycross on 24 May 1948. The Falcons won the match 57-38. (Norman Studios)

Above left: Australian Bonnie Waddell rode for Second Division Newcastle in 1947 and joined the Devils from Exeter in May 1948.

Above right: Plymouth riders Ivan Kessell, Len Read and Peter Robinson warming up their machines before a meeting. (M.E. Ness)

Below: Diminutive Len Read joined the Devils from Norwich in August 1947. After struggling to hold a place in the team in the early weeks of 1948, he finished with 344 points. (Norman Studios)

Above: Len Read going outside Poole's Sid Clark in heat six of the National League match at Wimborne Road on 14 June 1948. Read won the race in 84.4 seconds with Clark second and Peter Robinson third. (Norman Studios)

Below: In heat seven of the same meeting, Pete Lansdale drives inside Poole's George Gower. Lansdale went on to win in 83.6 seconds from Gower and Bonnie Waddell. The Devils had a superb 46–37 victory. (Norman Studios)

Left: Alex Gray took over the captaincy of the Devils from Billy Newell at the end of April but was badly injured at Hull on 10 July and missed several matches. Peter Robinson became the new skipper and continued to lead the team when Gray had recovered.

Below: Alex Gray always looked comfortable on a bike. Here he is seen practising at Southampton's Banister Court.

Opposite below: The Lord Mayor, Alderman H.J. Perry, shows the Plymouth riders that he can handle a speedway bike. From left to right: Alex Gray, Pete Lansdale, Len Read, Freddie Frape (team manager), Alderman Perry, Ted Gibson, Peter Robinson (captain), Vic Gent, Bonnie Waddell. (Devon Commercial Photos)

Above: Plymouth's Len Read in a close encounter with Poole's Joe Bowkis in the Devils' 48–36 league win over the Pirates on 17 June 1948. Read and Bowkis top scored for their respective teams with 11 points each. (Norman Studios)

Plymouth's Peter Robinson leads teammate Len Read, outside, and Cradley Heath's Eric Irons in heat eleven of the National League match on 8 July 1948. Robinson won in 82.6 seconds with Gil Craven second and Irons third. The Devils won the match 43-40. (Norman Studios)

Plymouth's Bonnie Waddell challenges Craven for the lead in heat fourteen of the clash on 8 July with Cradley Heath's Bill Clifton at the rear. Craven won in 83.6 seconds with Clifton second and Waddell third. (Norman Studios)

Len Read is presented with the Plymouth Royal Air Force Association Battle of Britain Silver Helmet on 16 September 1948 and is congratulated by runner-up Vic Emms of Coventry. (Devon Commercial Photos)

Plymouth team, 1948. From left to right, back row: Gordon Parkins (track manager), Alex Gray, Bonnie Waddell, Pete Lansdale, Ted Gibson, Len Read, Freddie Frape (team manager). Front row: Vic Gent, Wally Matthews, Peter Robinson (captain), Ivan Kessell. (Norman Studios)

Left: Ex-England international full-back Fred Titmuss joined Plymouth Argyle from Southampton in February 1926 for a record fee of £1,750. He gave six years' good service to Argyle and on retirement became a licensee. Titmuss ran the Cherry Tree pub which was next to Pennycross Stadium and for several of the post-war years provided a trophy for which the riders competed.

Below: Len Read receives the Cherry Tree tankard from Mrs Fred Titmuss for being the highest Plymouth scorer in the Plymouth-Exeter league match on 28 September 1948. Looking on is track manager Gordon Parkins, with Len's young son on his bike. (Devon Commercial Photos)

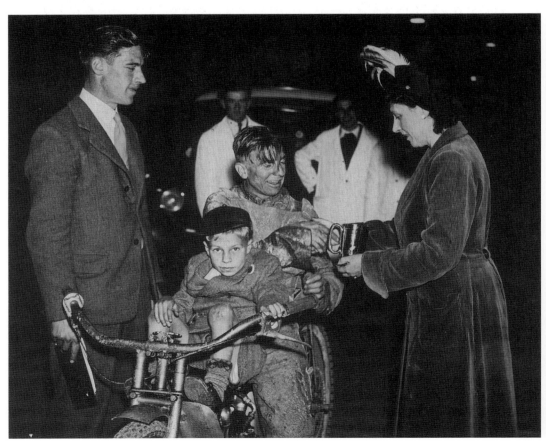

Pennycross favourite number five: Pete Lansdale. Born in London in 1912, Lansdale joined Southampton in 1947 after a successful career on the grass and in TT racing before the war. After signing for the Devils in 1948 he was a big scorer for the Pennycross side for six seasons. Billy Bales and he were the top two in the Division Three rankings in 1949 with Lansdale getting fourteen maximums. His Plymouth career was interrupted for a year in 1951 when he rode for Second Division Walthamstow and was their top scorer with 245 points. On his return to Plymouth he faced competition for the number-one spot from Alan Smith and George Wall but remained a very reliable points gatherer. Lansdale is the Devils' all-time highest scorer with 1,546 league points.

Above left: Tom Haughins acted as speedway track manager and clerk of the course as well as being the greyhound racing manager at Pennycross Stadium in 1949.

Above right: Alan Briggs took over from Phil Day as chief mechanic in April 1948 and also acted as team manager on occasions.

Pennycross Stadium, 1949. The main seated grandstand and the starting gate are on the left of the track with the covered standing enclosure on the opposite side. The dressing rooms, supporters' club hut and the totalisator are in the left foreground, with the uncovered pits area in front of the totalisator. The greyhound track is on the outside of the speedway track. The views from all parts of the stadium were good, especially from the banked areas on the bends. (Fitzgerald, Plymouth)

Above left: Hampshire-born Johnny Bradford joined Plymouth from Southampton in April 1949 and was making good progress until fracturing his skull on 14 September 1950. He recovered well and had a good 1951 season, but after a poor start to the next season moved to St Austell.

Above right: Skipper Peter Robinson partnered Bradford and was influential in his development.

Plymouth Devils line-up at Rayleigh on 11 June 1949 before their big 56–27 victory over the Rockets. From left to right, back row: Bonnie Waddell, Johnny Bradford, Pete Lansdale, Alan Smith. Front row: Peter Robinson (captain), Ivan Kessell, George Wall, Len Read. Read scored a 12-point maximum, with Robinson and Lansdale getting 11 points apiece.

Plymouth's Len Read leads in heat two of the league match at Rayleigh on 11 June 1949, followed by, from left to right, Ron Howes (Rayleigh), teammate Alan Smith and Charlie Mugford (Rayleigh). Read won in a time of 76.6 seconds, followed by Smith and Howes.

The Devils' captain Peter Robinson leads Buddy Fuller (Hastings) and Johnny Bradford in heat ten of the league match on 21 July 1949. That was how the race finished with Robinson winning in 80.6 seconds. The Saxons, however, won the match 43-40.

Above left: Alan Smith began his successful career with the Plymouth Devils in 1949.

Above right: Smith's first partner was Len Read, who played a big part in his development with his unselfish team riding.

A big crowd watch Plymouth pair Len Read, on the inside, and Alan Smith race closely together on the first bend at Pennycross Stadium. (Norman Studios)

Plymouth stars Pete Lansdale and Peter Robinson lead Tamworth's Harry Saunders in a Best Pairs meeting at Rayleigh's Weir Stadium.

Plymouth team, 1949. From left to right, standing: Tom Haughins (track manager), Bob Wigg, Jimmy Baxter (promoter). On machines: Geoff Woodger, Ivan Kessell, Peter Robinson (captain), Alan Smith, George Wall. Kneeling: Len Read, Johnny Bradford, Pete Lansdale, Toby Boshoff. (Norman Studios)

Pennycross favourite number six: Len Read. Born in Norwich on 8 January 1918, Read started on the track with his home-town club in 1946. He was making steady progress when he broke his leg in the second meeting at The Firs in 1947. Out of action for months and out of the picture at Norwich, Read signed for Plymouth in the August of that year. After experimenting with different frames, he became one of the top points scorers in 1948. His team riding with Alan Smith over the next two seasons was a feature of the racing at Pennycross. In 1951 Read moved with Peter Robinson to Jimmy Baxter's track at Liverpool when the Devils were demoted to Division Three. After two seasons on Merseyside he returned to the West Country track for the 1953 season. Read is the fourth highest scorer for the Devils, with 1,153 league points.

IVAN KESSELL

BILLY NEWELL

CHARLIE CHALLIS

STAN LANFEAR

GEOFF WOODGER

ALEX GRAY

BONNIE WADDELL

DOUG BELL

Above and opposite: Pennycross personalities from the 1940s. (Various publications)

PETE LANSDALE

PETER ROBINSON

LEN READ

GORDON PARKINS

FREDDIE FRAPE

JIMMY BAXTER

ALAN SMITH

JOHNNY BRADFORD

GEORGE WALL

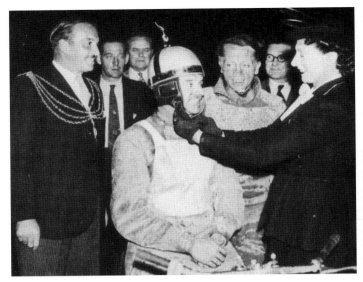

The Deputy Lady Mayoress of Plymouth, Mrs Trebilcock, presents the Plymouth Royal Air Force Association Battle of Britain Silver Helmet to Pete Lansdale on 15 September 1949. Peter Robinson receives an engraved silver tankard for being the runner-up. (*Western Morning News*)

The 1950 Plymouth team which beat Cradley Heath 50-34 in a challenge match in the first home fixture of the season on 7 April. From left to right, standing: Bob Wigg, Johnny Bradford, Len Read, Freddie Frape (team manager), Peter Robinson (captain), Geoff Woodger, Pete Lansdale, Alan Smith. On machines: Ivan Kessell, George Wall. Ivan Kessell scored 3 points in what was his last appearance for the Devils.

Plymouth's George Wall on the outside of Walthamstow's Dick Shepherd in the South Shield contest at Chingford Road on 24 April 1950. Both Wall and Shepherd, who was on Plymouth's books in 1947, scored 4 points in the match, which the Wolves won 51-33.

Plymouth team, 1950. From left to right, back row: Cecil Bailey, Jimmy Baxter (promoter), Alan Smith, Peter Bantock (director), Pete Lansdale, Bill Thatcher. Front row: George Wall, Peter Robinson (captain), Len Read, Johnny Bradford.

Above left and right: Two new signings from Southampton in 1950 were Cecil Bailey (*left*) and Bill Thatcher. Bailey returned to Banister Court after a few months but Thatcher became a big favourite at Pennycross for five seasons.

Cecil Bailey had scored 615 league points for the Saints in the two previous seasons but could not reproduce that form for Plymouth.

Pennycross favourite number seven: Peter Robinson. Born in High Wycombe in 1919, Robinson had some pre-war outings at Rye House. He was signed by Wimbledon in 1946 but had a bad smash which put him out of action. Robinson went to Southampton in 1947 and reached double figures in twenty four of the thirty matches in which he rode. Wembley recruited him in 1948 but at the time his health would not allow him to cope with the rigours of Division One racing. Southampton wanted him back but they had already signed Alf Bottoms so Jimmy Baxter took him to Plymouth. Robinson's white-line riding was very effective and once he had settled at Pennycross he became a powerful scorer and an inspirational captain. Robinson is the all-time fifth highest scorer for the Devils with 955 points.

Above left: Former Exeter captain Bronco Slade rode a few matches for the Devils at the end of 1950 and the beginning of 1951 with little success and soon moved on to St Austell. (Bick and Searle)

Above right: Peter Robinson in action for the Southern Stars at Walthamstow on 12 June 1950, where he and Len Read scored 7 points each but could not prevent the Wolves winning 46–35.

Plymouth team, 1950. From left to right, back row: Freddie Frape (team manager), Alan Smith, Dennis Hayles, Wally Mawdsley, Jimmy Baxter (promoter), Pete Lansdale, Bill Thatcher, Johnny Bradford, Alan Briggs (chief mechanic). Front row: George Wall, Peter Robinson (captain, on machine), Len Read. (Norman Studios)

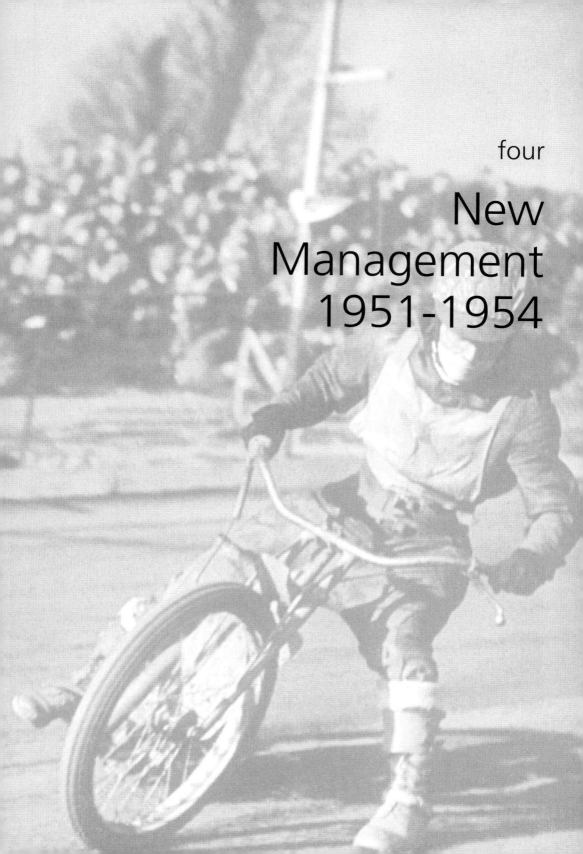

four

New Management 1951-1954

Above: Two newcomers from Poole in 1951. *Left:* Frank Holcombe had fourteen outings in Devils' colours in May and June without ever reaching a double-figure score. *Right:* Frank Wheeler arrived in July and became a regular in the Plymouth team until early in the 1953 season.

Above left: Local rider Brian Hitchcock joined in 1951 after some experience at Exeter, and scored two maximums in his first season. He showed great promise but never fulfilled his considerable potential.

Above right: A product of the Speedway World Training School, Tom Turnham rode for Liverpool before coming to Pennycross in 1951.

Plymouth team, 1951. From left to right, standing: George Craig, Brian Hitchcock, Bill Thatcher, Tom Turnham, Dennis Hayles, Johnny Bradford. On machines: George Wall (captain), Alan Smith.

First-bend action in heat four of the Plymouth-Wolverhampton league match at Pennycross on 28 June 1951. From left to right: George Craig (Plymouth), John Hitchings (Wolverhampton), Dennis Hayles (Plymouth) and Jack Cunningham (Wolverhampton). Hitchings won in 77 seconds from Cunningham, Craig and Hayles to give the Wasps their only race win in the Devils' big 61-23 victory.

Above left: Ron Barrett came on loan from Harringay in August and was an ever-present in the side, scoring a maximum at St Austell on 25 September.

Above right: Thirty-seven-year-old George Craig joined from Swindon and was a solid second string, adding experience to the line-up.

Plymouth's Alan Smith leading Trevor Redmond, with Kiwi Bob McFarlane holding off Swindon's Buster Brown in heat fourteen of the Junior Test match between England 'C' and New Zealand at Ipswich on 19 July 1951. Smith and McFarlane both fell, leaving Redmond to win from Brown. New Zealand were victorious 57-50 in front of a 13,792 crowd.

Pennycross favourite number eight: Alan Smith. Born at Forest Gate, London in 1928, Smith
started riding at the Speedway World Training School in October 1948. Jimmy Baxter
gave him a trial at Banister Court the following March, signed him and allocated him to
Pennycross. He made good progress in 1949 as a second string to Len Read, continued his
development the following year and by 1951 was the Devils' top scorer. Smith also finished
at the head of the Division Three averages and was runner-up in the Third Division Riders'
Championship final at Cardiff. He rode for England 'C' and in 1952 George Wall and he
were the top two in the Southern League. Smith was coveted by many First Division tracks
and when the Devils closed in 1954 he was signed by West Ham, the team he supported as a
boy. Smith is the all-time second highest Plymouth scorer with 1,280 points.

Plymouth team, 1952. From left to right: Alan Smith, Dennis Hayles, Bill Thatcher, Frank Wheeler, George Wall (captain, on machine), Doug Fursey, Bill Rundle, Brian Hitchcock, Johnny Bradford, Pete Lansdale, Sid Hazzard (team manager).

Plymouth skipper George Wall and Exeter's Vic Gent fight for the lead in heat six of the National Trophy match at the County Ground on 28 April 1952. Wall went on to win in 75.1 seconds from Gent, new Falcon Ron Barrett and Bill Thatcher. Exeter won the match 57-51.

Above left: Doug Fursey was a regular second string for Plymouth from 1951 to 1953, making seventy-nine appearances. He had some second-half rides at Exeter in 1954 but was unable to gain a place in the team.

Above right: Dennis Hayles joined the Devils from Southampton halfway through 1950 and held his place in the side until June 1952 when he returned to Banister Court.

Above left: Sydney-born Ted Stevens arrived at Pennycross from Wolverhampton in June 1952 and showed great promise until tragically killed at St Austell on 12 April 1953.

Above right: Cornishman Bill Rundle had some experience at Exeter and St Austell before making spasmodic appearances for the Devils in 1952.

Above: With Smith and Wall on World Championship duty, Exeter's Goog Hoskin (*left*) and Swindon's Bob Jones (*right*) guested for Plymouth in a challenge match against Second Division Leicester on 29 May 1952. Hoskin scored a faultless maximum and equalled the track record of 72 seconds set up by Pete Lansdale in April. Leicester won the match 46–38.

One in, one out. Former Walthamstow boss John Deeley, left, became team manager of the Devils in June 1952, releasing Sid Hazzard to concentrate on mechanical matters. In August, Pete Lansdale, who Deeley had taken to Chingford Road in 1951, temporarily retired from the track.

Above left: The programme for the England 'C' *v.* Sweden match at Pennycross on 24 July 1952. England were captained by Devils' skipper George Wall, who scored 11 points. The result was a 54-54 draw and the meeting was watched by nearly 10,000.

Above right: Plymouth's Alan Smith top scored for the England side with a brilliant 14 points.

Plymouth team, 1952. From left to right, back row: Bill Rundle, Alan Smith, John Deeley (team manager), Doug Fursey, Brian Hitchcock. Front row: Ted Stevens, George Wall (captain, with team mascot), Frank Wheeler, Bill Thatcher.

Above: George Wall (*left*) and Alan Smith (*right*) topped the Southern League averages in 1952 with 10.4 and 10.2 points respectively.

Rider	Team	M.	P.	B.	T.	P.M.	A.
G. WALL	Plymouth	36	374	3	377	18	10.4
A. Smith	Plymouth	38	382	6	388	15	10.2
J. Unstead	Rayleigh	38	336	24	360	10	9.4
G. Jackson	Rayleigh	37	331	16	347	10	9.3
P. Lansdale	Plymouth	23	205	11	216	10	9.3
G. Hoskin	Exeter	33	295	6	301	7	9.1
S. Clark	Ipswich	38	334	12	346	5	9.1
P. Clark	Rayleigh	36	289	33	322	11	8.9
C. May	Cardiff	36	286	34	320	11	8.8
B. King	Wolv'ton	34	284	14	298	9	8.7
G. Pugh	Cardiff	39	296	36	322	9	8.5
M. Holland	Cardiff	38	280	39	319	9	8.3
M. McDermott	Rayleigh	38	285	32	317	9	8.3
B. Thatcher	Plymouth	37	274	36	310	4	8.3
H. Geddes	Cardiff	39	289½	32	321½	5	8.2
B. McKeown	Southampton	31	236	17	253	4	8.1
T. O'Connor	Rayleigh	37	255	46	301	2	8.1
I. Powell	Aldershot	37	279	17	296	6	8.0
C. Quick	Wolv'ton	37	282	14	296	6	8.0
C. Taylor	Cardiff	39	278	33	311	8	7.9
F. Evans	Swindon	37	276	16	292	6	7.8
V. Gent	Exeter	38	268	26	294	4	7.7
N. Street	St. Austell	37	274½	12	286½	2	7.7
A. Quinn	St. Austell	38	281	15	296	5	7.7
B. Croucher	Southampton	32	229	15	244	3	7.6
D. Hardy	Exeter	24	174	6	180	2	7.5

In 1951, Alan Smith headed the Third Division league averages. In 1952 he was again in brilliant form but was just pipped for the honour of being top man in the Southern League by his team mate George Wall. Several First Division clubs were interested in the Plymouth pair but both Smith and Wall seemed happy to stay at Pennycross.

Pennycross favourite number nine: George Wall. Born in London in 1922, Wall learned how to ride a speedway bike at Rye House. He was signed by Jimmy Baxter and originally allocated to Liverpool but he wanted to go to Plymouth with Alan Smith so Baxter moved Alex Gray to the Stanley Stadium instead. When Peter Robinson went to Liverpool at the end of the 1950 season, Wall became the Devils' new skipper. He led the team well and gained a regular place in the England 'C' side. He suffered serious injury in a pre-season crash in 1953 and was advised to hang up his leathers. He ignored the advice but Wall was never quite the same again. After six seasons at Pennycross he is the Devils' third highest scorer with 1,170 points.

FATAL ACCIDENT TO AUSTRALIAN RIDER

SECOND fatality on British tracks this season occurred at St. Austell on Tuesday of last week, when 26-year-old Australian Ted Stevens lost his life during the St. Austell v. Plymouth Southern League match.

The crash happened at a bend. St. Austell rider Ken Monk fell and Stevens, unable to avoid him, was catapulted into a lamp standard. Stevens was taken to hospital, where he died.

Monk sustained concussion, while a third rider involved, Jackie Gates, escaped with a shaking.

Above left: Popular Australian Ted Stevens was a big loss to the Pennycross supporters both on and off the track.

Above right: Dick Howard, ex-Hanley and Poole, had a few outings in the first month of the 1953 season before becoming a Falcon at Exeter.

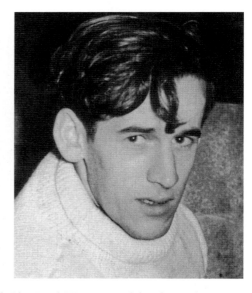

Above left: Former Wolverhampton and St Austell rider Derek Timms signed for Plymouth in May 1953 and was a regular member of the team in that season.

Above right: New Zealander Kevin Hayden, the former Cardiff heat leader, joined the Devils after the Dragons closed in July 1953. He had fractured both arms at the end of 1951 but slowly regained his confidence at Pennycross.

Above left: Edinburgh's Harold Fairhurst won the Plymouth World Championship round on 29 May 1953 with a 15-point maximum. In his first race he lowered the track record to 71.6 seconds.

Above right: George Wall was still trying to regain his form after his pre-season accident but improved as the meeting went on and finished with 8 points.

Plymouth team, 1953. From left to right, standing: Stan Clark, Pete Lansdale, Alan Smith, Jack Bridson, Dick Harris, Bill Thatcher. Front row: George Wall (captain, on machine), Kevin Hayden, Len Read.

Above left: Pete Lansdale returned to Pennycross for the 1953 season and was a welcome addition to the Devils' ranks.

Above right: Old favourite Len Read also came back to Plymouth after two years away at Liverpool.

The start of heat three in the league clash between the Devils and the Falcons at the County Ground on 6 July 1953. From left to right, Jack Geran, Derek Timms, Neil Street and Bill Thatcher get away from the gate. Plymouth's Thatcher won the race in 74.3 seconds from Geran, Street and Timms but Exeter won the meeting 59-25.

Pennycross favourite number ten: Bill Thatcher. After getting some experience at the Speedway World Training School and on the Continent, New Zealand-born Thatcher made his league debut for Southampton in May 1949. He made regular appearances as reserve for the Saints that season. Jimmy Baxter moved him to Plymouth in 1950 where he made steady progress until he was hurt in September. His 1951 season also ended early when he had a serious knee injury in July. However, in 1952 Thatcher became a heat leader when Pete Lansdale retired. He put some big scores together, finishing with 254 league points. He was in great form again the following year until he fractured his skull at his old track at Banister Court. Showing typical Thatcher grit and determination he was racing again in a few weeks. Bill Thatcher's easygoing, cheerful personality endeared him to the Plymouth speedway public and he was one of the most popular riders ever to appear at Pennycross Stadium.

Above left: Stan Clark joined the Devils on loan from Harringay in June 1953 and gave excellent support to the heat leaders.

Above right: County Ground favourite Johnny Sargeant wanted to go to a flat track so he also joined Plymouth in June. He struggled at Pennycross and moved further west to St Austell after a few weeks.

At the age of forty-one, famous speedway pioneer Phil Bishop made one appearance for Plymouth at Liverpool in a Queen's Cup match on 15 June 1953. As wild and unpredictable as ever, he fell on the first corner in heat four, bringing down partner Johnny Sargeant, but managed a point in his second race.

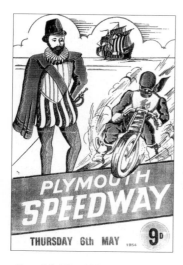

Above left: The 1954 programme cover was designed by fourteen-year-old Plymouth schoolboy Ray Finn. He sent it to the speedway management, who decided to use it. Coloured red, yellow and black, it had an image of Sir Francis Drake, an Armada ship and a speedway rider.

Above right: Bill Thatcher missed the first four matches of the 1954 season as he had not returned from New Zealand in time.

This Plymouth team lost 45-39 to Ipswich in a challenge match in the first home meeting of the 1954 season on 16 April. From left to right: Dick Harris, Harold Bull, Jackie Gates, George Wall (captain, on machine), Ken Holmes, Kevin Hayden, Alan Smith, Pete Lansdale, Don Weekes (team manager).

Above: St Austell's top two riders, Australians Harold Bull (*left*) and Jackie Gates, joined the Devils for the 1954 season and much was expected of them. Bull managed the occasional good score but Gates struggled and at one stage lost his place in the side.

Above left: Young New Zealander Hec Mayhead, who was signed from Wembley, showed great determination and aggression in his riding and made a big impression in his short time at Pennycross.

Above right: Ken Holmes, on loan from Wimbledon, looked full of promise but got injured and lost confidence.

Above: Alan Smith (*left*) and Pete Lansdale, who were both in their sixth season in Plymouth's colours, were again the best riders at Pennycross.

Action from the Southern Shield match between Plymouth and Southampton at Pennycross on 22 April 1954 with Plymouth's Alan Smith on the inside of Southampton's Ernie Brecknell. The Devils won 44–39 with each rider top scoring for his team, Smith getting a 12-point maximum and Brecknell scoring 9 points.

A strong-looking 1954 Plymouth squad. From left to right, back row: Cyril Gray (promoter), Jackie Gates, Alan Smith, Don Weekes (team manager), George Wall (captain), Bill Thatcher, Kevin Hayden, Freddie Frape (track manager). Front row: Harold Bull, Kevin Bock, Hec Mayhead, Ken Holmes, Pete Lansdale.

Above left: Thirty-five-year-old Vic Gent returned home to Pennycross after five seasons at Exeter where he scored 946 league points. His last match for the Falcons was against the Devils in the Devon Derby at the County Ground on 17 May 1954.

Above right: The winner of the final meeting at Pennycross in 1954 was Southampton's Brian McKeown, who won the Plymouth World Championship round on 8 July with a brilliant 15-point maximum.

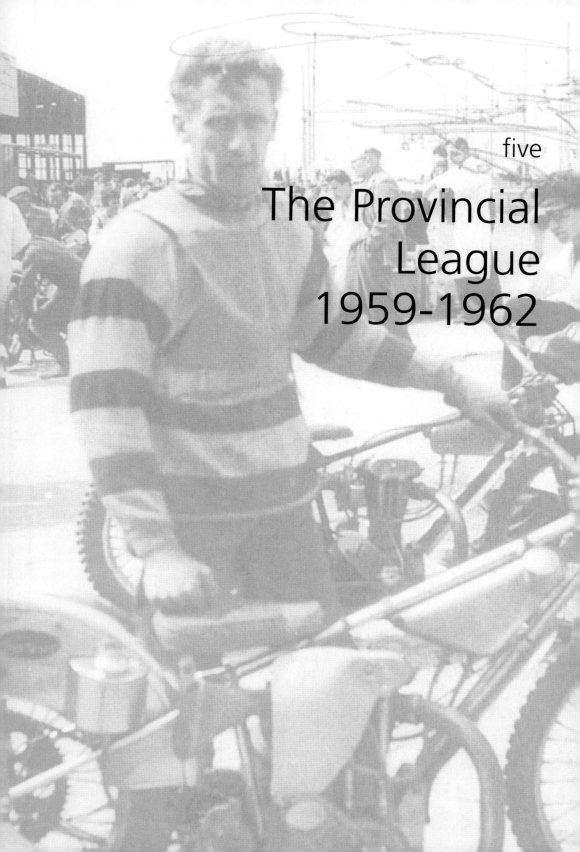

five

The Provincial League 1959-1962

Above left: England international and world finalist Split Waterman led the Devils in the first speedway seen at Pennycross for five years.

Above right: Former Wembley rider Trevor Redmond, together with Eric Netcott of Western Promotions, put on five meetings at Plymouth in 1959.

Grand opening SPEEDWAY

" WEST OF ENGLAND MATCH RACE "

Pete Lansdale (Plymouth) v. Trevor Redmond (St. Austell)

DEVILS v. MIDLANDS, including **sensational SPLIT WATERMAN**

★ALAN SMITH ★RAY CRESP ★HARRY BASTABLE ★JACK UNSTEAD
★LES McGILLIVRAY, etc.

PLYMOUTH SPORTS STADIUM

GOOD FRIDAY
3-15 p.m.

Admission 3/-, 4/-. Reserved 5/-
Children 1/-, 2/-. Reserved 2/6

Telephone 71247

✦ WIN PREMIUM BONDS on Lucky Programme & Car Park

The 'Grand Opening' advertisement for the meeting on Good Friday 27 March 1959 was featured in the local *Evening Herald*.

Right: 1954 and 1959 World Champion Ronnie Moore, of Wimbledon, was unbeaten in his team's Best Pairs victory at Pennycross on 23 April 1959. Moore came to this country as a seventeen-year-old in 1950 and in that season scored nearly 200 points for the Dons, rode for the Australian Test team and became the youngest rider to appear in the World Championship final. Twenty-one years later, in 1971, he made his last final appearance.

Below: Peter Craven, World Champion in 1955 and 1962, skippered the Devils to a 54-42 victory over Oxford on 15 May 1959 with a 15-point maximum. He also established a new Pennycross track record of 70.6 seconds which has never been beaten.

Above: Southampton's Geoff Mardon (*left*) and Leicester's Ken McKinlay top scored for the Combined Stars' team on 7 July 1959 in a pulsating 48-48 draw with the Swedish Lions.

Above: The 1960 Poole team represented Plymouth against Bristol on 8 September in a match drawn 36–36. Tony Lewis (*left*) and Ross Gilbertson scored 10 apiece for the Plymouth side.

Right: Rayleigh's Eric Hockaday won a Provincial League Riders' Championship qualifying round at Pennycross on 15 September 1960 with a 15-point maximum. Four days later he scored another maximum, this time for Exeter in a challenge match against Plymouth at the County Ground. A stylish rider, Hockaday captained the Exeter Falcons in their first season in the Provincial League in 1961.

Opposite: Ove Fundin (*left*) and Rune Sormander each scored 15 points for the Lions in a masterly display of speedway racing.

Above left: Former Bristol rider Eric Salmon, who promoted two meetings at Pennycross in 1960, introduced Provincial League racing to Plymouth in 1961.

Above right: The Plymouth team inherited Bristol's nickname and race jackets and one of the Bulldogs' best riders, Cliff Cox, became captain.

Plymouth team, 1961. From left to right: Chris Blewett, Frank Evans, Ray Wickett, Cliff Cox (captain, on machine), Jack Scott, Pat Flanagan, Ron Bagley, Chris Julian.

Above left: East Anglian Ron Bagley's bustling style and charges round the fence when he scored 14 points from eight exhausting rides in the first meeting against Poole on 31 March 1961, made him an instant hero with the 6,500 crowd.

Above right: In contrast, Ivor Toms rode his first and last race in 1961 when he fractured his leg in a heat-three crash. However, he recovered to become a regular in 1962.

Plymouth's Ron Bagley and Maury Mattingley lead Edinburgh's Doug Templeton and Jimmy Tannock in heat two of the league clash at Pennycross on 4 August 1961. The race finished in that order with Bagley's time being 75.8 seconds. The Bulldogs won 46-32 with Bagley getting a brilliant 10 points.

Pennycross favourite number eleven: Jack Scott. Although Scott only had one season at Pennycross, his performances were such that he merits a place among the favourites. He arrived from Southampton at the beginning of 1961 after enjoying a big pools win in Australia in the winter. He improved his equipment and it showed. Scott got double figures in twenty-one out of twenty-five matches for the Bulldogs and his lowest score was 8. He held five Provincial League track records. Scott qualified for the British final of the World Championship and was also selected to ride for Great Britain against Sweden. 1961 was an outstanding year for the young Australian, who at last realised the potential everyone said he had and was idolised at Pennycross.

Above left: Veteran Bristolian Frank Evans was forty-six when he came to Plymouth with the Bulldogs in 1961. Tempted out of retirement at Knowle in 1960, his short stay at Pennycross yielded 2 points in four league matches.

Above right: Londoner Pat Flanagan actually had one challenge match outing with the Devils on 15 May 1953 and was another of the 1960 Bulldogs to come to Plymouth. A steady second string, he moved on to Newcastle in July 1961.

Above left: Young Cornishman Chris Julian was a most effective second string in 1961, frightening the opposition and notching some good scores.

Above right: Fellow Cornishman Ray Wickett had rides at several tracks before coming to Pennycross in 1961. He had ability but injury and mechanical problems hampered his progress.

Pennycross favourite number twelve: Maury Mattingley. Thirty-five-year-old Mattingley had six years at his home-town club Southampton and three at Coventry before making a huge impact at Pennycross in 1961. Able to ride all tracks, he was a big scorer home and away and he and Jack Scott formed a potent spearhead for the Bulldogs. To crown his season he was third in the Provincial League Riders' Championship final at Harringay. Mattingley started 1962 with a succession of high scores but was affected by injury and missed several matches in the second half of the season.

The top three at the Provincial League Riders' Championship final at Harringay on 16 September 1961. From left to right: Maury Mattingley (Plymouth), Trevor Redmond (Wolverhampton) and winner Reg Reeves (Rayleigh). Mattingley and Redmond finished with 12 points each and the Wolves rider beat the Bulldog in a run-off for second place.

Above left: The original 1962 programme was printed in London by Talent Advertising Limited. Because of delivery problems, it was replaced halfway through the season by local firm E.J. Rickard Limited.

Above right: New promoter Bernard Curtiss got off to a good start by reinstating the Devils' nickname and race jacket and putting together an attractive team for the 1962 season.

Plymouth team, 1962. From left to right, back row: Maury Mattingley, Cliff Cox (captain), Bernard Curtiss (promoter), Jimmy Squibb, Chris Julian, Ivor Toms. Front row: Len Glover (team manager), Bert Roger, Chris Blewett.

Left: The Devils had one of the strongest heat-leader trios in the Provincial League in 1962. From left to right: Maury Mattingley, Cliff Cox, Jimmy Squibb. (*Western Evening Herald*)

Opposite: Pennycross favourite number thirteen: Cliff Cox. Born in Bristol, Cox began his racing years at Knowle Stadium in the early 1950s. He was at Oxford in 1959 before rejoining the Bulldogs in the Provincial League in 1960. Third highest scorer behind Trevor Redmond and Johnny Hole, he moved to Plymouth with the Bristol promotion in 1961 and was appointed captain. A strong, fearless leader, he led by example, scoring well home and away. His good form continued in 1962 when he qualified for the Provincial League Riders' Championship final. After Plymouth closed he had an outstanding season at Exeter but early in 1964 he suffered a broken leg and other injuries in a bad crash, from which he never really recovered. However, he was persuaded out of retirement by promoter Fred Osborn and rode a few matches for the Devils in 1969.

Above left: Former England captain Bert Roger rode for half the season for the 1962 Devils and managed two maximums among his scores.

Above right: Promoter Curtiss caused some disquiet when he was allowed to sign Jimmy Squibb from National League Ipswich. However, he got away with it and Squibb proved to be an excellent replacement for 1961 star Jack Scott.

Action from heat four of the Devon Derby second leg between the Devils and the Falcons at the County Ground on 23 April 1962. Jimmy Squibb and Howdy Byford battle for the lead with Francis Cann and Ivor Toms at the back. Byford won in 78.4 seconds from Squibb, Cann and Toms. The match was drawn 39-39 but Plymouth won 82-74 on aggregate. (Bromley)

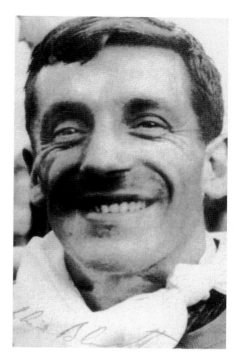

Above left and right: Canadian born Chris Blewett's 1961 season was marred by a terrible crash at Wolverhampton where he received severe facial injuries. In 1962, however, he made great progress with some outstanding heat-leader performances. In the final home meeting on 4 October, Blewett was beaten by Jimmy Squibb in a run-off in the Westward Television Champion of Champions meeting after both riders had scored 14 points.

Leaving the gate in heat three of the Southern League meeting at Wimborne Road on 9 May 1962. From left to right: Tim Bungay (Poole), George Summers (Plymouth), Bobby Croombs (Poole) and Bert Roger (Plymouth). Bungay won in 75.6 seconds from Croombs, Summers and Roger. Poole won the match 51-26.

Above: Two of the strongest riders at Pennycross in the two Provincial League seasons were Cliff Cox (*left*) and Chris Julian. Often paired together, their aggressive style made them a formidable combination.

The 1962 Plymouth team that was tracked towards the end of the season. From left to right: Chris Julian, Bernard Curtiss (promoter), Jimmy Squibb, Cliff Cox (captain, on machine), George Summers, Chris Blewett, Cy Melville (team manager), Ivor Toms, Lew Philp.

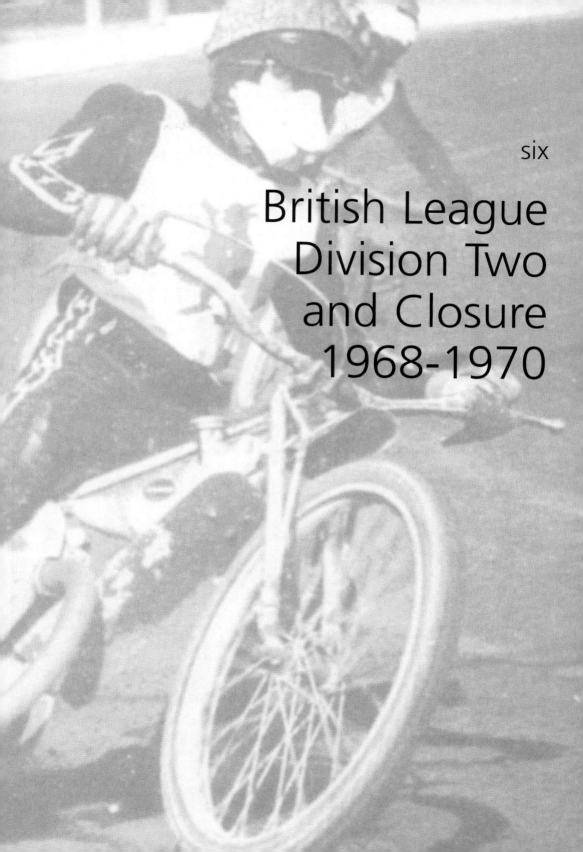

six

British League Division Two and Closure 1968-1970

Above left: Local businessman and stadium manager Fred Osborn worked with Pete Lansdale in 1968 but promoted speedway on his own for the final two seasons at Pennycross. He deserves great credit for his efforts in what were difficult circumstances.

Above right: The 1968 programme was printed by Rayleigh Press Limited and coloured red, black and white.

Plymouth team, 1968. From left to right: Frank Payne, Keith Marks, Bill Cake (team manager), Phil Woodcock, Mike Cake (captain, on machine), Chris Roynon, Tony George, Dave Whitaker. (Wright Wood)

Above left: The Devils' captain Mike Cake in action.

Above right: At twenty-eight years of age, Australian Chris Bass was the oldest rider in the 1968 Plymouth team. He and Mike Cake were two of the best performers in the Second Division.

Plymouth's Phil Woodcock challenges Reading's Ian Champion on the first bend of heat one of the league match at Tilehurst on 24 June 1968. Woodcock later fell and Champion won from the Devils' Chris Roynon and Ian Bottomley. The Racers won the match 50-28.

Above left: Twenty-two-year-old Bristolian Chris Roynon was a steady-scoring second string in all three seasons that he rode at Pennycross.

Above right: Frank Payne showed promise in 1968 and his scores included a maximum at home to Rayleigh on 9 August. The next day he suffered a hairline fracture of the skull at Nelson and only had a few more outings at the beginning of 1969.

Bristol-born Tony George learned the basics of speedway at Weymouth under the tutelage of Lew Coffin. Only seventeen and a half, he was signed by Exeter and loaned to the Devils for the 1968 season. George had an exciting style and was an ever-present for Plymouth in his first year of league racing.

Pennycross favourite number fourteen: Mike Cake. Born in Parkstone, Dorset in 1946, Cake was on loan from Exeter in 1968. He was appointed captain and had a brilliant season in the Second Division. So well did he do that he also rode twenty-eight matches in the senior division with the Falcons. Cake had sixteen double-figure scores in twenty-two matches for the Devils and was top qualifier for the Division Two Riders' Championship final at Hackney. It was inevitable that he would ride in the First Division in 1969. After he left Pennycross, Cake had a further year at the County Ground followed by four seasons at his local track at Wimborne Road.

Above left: Fifty-six-year-old Hampshire-born George Newton was the Devils' coach in 1969. The pre-war England star's last club as a rider was St Austell, for whom he rode in 1952. Based in Cornwall, Newton acted as team manager for home meetings.

Above right: Ian Gills, another Devil from Bristol, had an injury-hit two years at Pennycross before moving to Romford in August 1969. (Alf Weedon)

Twenty-three-year-old New Zealander Dave Whitaker rode for Plymouth for two seasons and was captain in 1969. He got many high scores on his home track but was not so effective away. Whitaker was selected as reserve for New Zealand against England at Swindon on 6 August and was the only Second Division rider to take part in the match.

Above: After weeks of speculation, former Plymouth captain Cliff Cox was welcomed back to Pennycross by promoter Fred Osborn on 4 July 1969. His presence inspired the Devils to a big 49-29 victory over Rayleigh, although he failed to score. (*Western Evening Herald*)

Opposite below: Plymouth team, 1969. From left to right, back row: Colin Sanders, Keith Marks, Graham Hambly (team manager), Chris Roynon, Adrian Degan. Front row: Dave Whitaker (captain), John Hammond, Bob Coles.

Pennycross favourite number fifteen: Colin Sanders. Born in Poole in 1949, Sanders' achievements in his first year of speedway were remarkable. After a couple of second-half outings he made his debut on 9 May 1969 and scored a swashbuckling 10 points in the 40-38 win over Crayford. Three weeks later Sanders scored his first maximum in a challenge match victory over Reading. That was the first of six maximums at Pennycross that season. He qualified for the Division Two Riders' Championship final at Hackney in September. Sanders also broke the Pennycross Division Two track record with a time of 79.2 seconds in the first heat of the Rayleigh match on 4 July. Although still on Plymouth's books, he had two seasons at Romford in 1970 and 1971 before seemingly disappearing from the track as quickly as he had arrived.

Above left: Keith Marks, from Dorset, was a promising second string who had a long spell out of the team in 1968 but was very consistent in his second season at Pennycross.

Above right: John Hammond top scored for Weymouth at Pennycross in 1968. Fred Osborn remembered and snapped him up the next season. Hammond made his debut for the Devils on 23 May 1969. Fairly low scores followed but he got his first maximum against Newport Colts in the last home meeting of 1969. Hammond returned to Plymouth for the open season and was also a regular at Reading.

Around 3,000 saw Eastbourne visit Pennycross on 4 April in the first meeting of the 1969 season. Here, on the first bend in heat one, the visitors' Barry Crowson is ahead of Chris Roynon, Laury Sims and Ian Gills. Moments later Sims hit the fence and came down. The race was rerun and Crowson won in 84.2 seconds from Roynon and Gills. The Devils won the match 41-37.

Pennycross favourite number sixteen: Bob Coles. Born in Exeter in 1944, Coles had three league outings in 1968. Starting as reserve the following year, he made rapid progress and finished second highest scorer behind Colin Sanders. He ended the season with an unbeaten six rides when he collected the Bromley Bowl on 3 October. Popular with supporters for his wholehearted performances, Coles returned in 1970 to reach double figures in seven of the nine matches in which he rode. He also made thirty-six appearances for the Falcons. His apprenticeship at Pennycross served him well for he went on to ride for many clubs in a long career.

seven

Results and Scorers

1932
National Association Trophy/National League

Belle Vue	(H)	25-28 /	23-25
Belle Vue	(A)	18-36 /	15-35
Coventry	(H)	34-20 /	31-22
Coventry	(A)	23-28 /	18-34
Crystal Palace	(H)	16-37 /	19-35
Crystal Palace	(A)	19-35 /	20-31
Sheffield	(H)	39-14	★
Sheffield	(A)	17-37	★
Soton/Clapton	(H)	16-34 /	33-20
Clapton	(A)	16-37 /	18-36
Stamford Bridge	(H)	26-27 /	30-22
Stamford Bridge	(A)	12-39 /	15-39
Wembley	(H)	15-36 /	16-35
Wembley	(A)	16-36 /	24-27
West Ham	(H)	20-33 /	32-18
West Ham	(A)	15-34 /	20-34
Wimbledon	(H)	24-28 /	22-29
Wimbledon	(A)	13-34 /	20½-33½

★ Sheffield did not compete in the National League.

Scorers (Trophy and League): B. Clibbett 167½, B. Spencer 115, E. Collins 112, J. Jackson 75, F. Pearce 73, F. Goulden 46, S. Lupton 40, C. Mitchell 22, J. Barber 18, P. Slade 16, R. Taylor 14, B. Ellmore 9, B. Jones 8, F. Hawken 4, T. MacDonald 3, A. Humphreys 3, A. Warren 2, A. Summersby 1, J Ewing 0.

1933
National League

Belle Vue	(H)	34-29	21-42
Belle Vue	(A)	19-44	11-52
Clapton	(H)	20-42	24-38
Clapton	(A)	23-40	18-45
Coventry	(H)	38-21	18-45
Coventry	(A)	45-18	12-51
Crystal Palace	(H)	33-30	30-32
Crystal Palace	(A)	17-45	22-41
Nottingham	(H)	46-16	36-23
Nottingham	(A)	17-45	21-40
Sheffield	(H)	32-31	31-30
Sheffield	(A)	31-32	25-38
Wembley	(H)	34-29	35-27
Wembley	(A)	17-46	15-48
West Ham	(H)	32-31	21-42
West Ham	(A)	22-40	23-40
Wimbledon	(H)	31-32	30-33
Wimbledon	(A)	23-38	15-47

Scorers: B. Clibbett 179, J. Sharp 151, B. Stanley 116, T. Bravery 110, F. Goulden 97, B. Spencer 65, R. Stanley 62, S. Roth 55, J. Glass 52, J. Jackson 14, H. Bray 10, B. Living 8, A. Summersby 2, F. Hawken 1.

1934
National League

Belle Vue	(H)	18-36	31-22
Belle Vue	(A)	0-36	12-41
Hall Green	(H)	32-20	30-23
Hall Green	(A)	23-31	14-39
Harringay	(H)	26-26	28-26
Harringay	(A)	15-35	14-40
Lea Bridge	(H)	29-22	25-28
Lea Bridge	(A)	25-28	31-22
New Cross	(H)	23-31	21-32
New Cross	(A)	22-31	9-42
Wembley	(H)	23-30	22-32
Wembley	(A)	14-40	12-41
West Ham	(H)	27-27	22-32
West Ham	(A)	11-40	14-40
Wimbledon	(H)	27-22	28-25
Wimbledon	(A)	20-33	20-34

Scorers: J. Sharp 164, B. Clibbett 113, F. Pearce 94, M. Murphy 82, P. Hart 73, B. Spencer 69, B. Stanley 40, L. Killmeyer 17, T. Bravery 16, I. Hill 1.

1936

Provincial League /	Trophy		
Bristol	(H)	35-37 /	46-25
Bristol	(H)	35-36 /	–
Bristol	(A)	32-40 /	22-50
Bristol	(A)	23-49 /	–
Cardiff	(H)	57-15 /	★
Cardiff	(H)	★ /	★
Cardiff	(A)	34-37 /	★
Cardiff	(A)	★ /	★
Liverpool	(H)	25-47 /	38-34
Liverpool	(H)	40-32 /	–
Liverpool	(A)	24-43 /	23-46
Liverpool	(A)	26-44 /	–
Nottingham	(H)	35-37 /	Not Run
Nottingham	(H)	27-44 /	–
Nottingham	(A)	32½-39½ /	33-38
Nottingham	(A)	23-48 /	–
Southampton	(H)	47-25 /	42-30
Southampton	(H)	29-43 /	–
Southampton	(A)	20-49 /	27-44
Southampton	(A)	23-49 /	–
West Ham Reserves	(H)	– /	53-18
West Ham Reserves	(A)	– /	34-34

★ Cardiff resigned from league and did not compete in trophy.

NB. Only 9 matches took place in trophy competition. Nottingham awarded points in match not run.

Scorers (League and Trophy): L. Bowden 152, D. Wise 148, J. Bibby 113, J. Hobson 85, B. Lamont 73, F. Tuck 71, L. Gregory 56, D. Hemmingway 40, S. Marsland 35½, J. Riddle 10, P. Byrne 4, C. Anderson 3, L. Keefe 1, F. Hemmingway 0.

1947
National League Division Three

Cradley Heath	(H)	40-42	45-33
Cradley Heath	(A)	30-54	22-62
Eastbourne	(H)	30-54	47-37
Eastbourne	(A)	27-56	29-52
Exeter	(H)	40-43	44-40
Exeter	(A)	28-55	30-53
Hanley	(H)	41-42	47-36
Hanley	(A)	23-59	20-63
Southampton	(H)	39-44	42-42
Southampton	(A)	34-49	22-62
Tamworth	(H)	41-43	44-40
Tamworth	(A)	38-44	29-54
Wombwell	(H)	43-40	54-29
Wombwell	(A)	30-54	36-48

Scorers: I. Kessell 186, S. Lanfear 154, A. Gray 134, C. Challis 128, B. Newell 110, H. Sharp 51, V. Gent 47, D. Bell 43, L. Read 40, B. Deegan 20, J. Cashmore 19, L. Covell 16, R. Westwood 14, J. Milross 11, B. Sale 8, D. Tamblin 6, K. Slee 3, V. Bernard 2, P. Day 2, L. Gore 1, G. Argrave 0, M. Hogan 0, D. Shepherd 0, B. Williams 0.

1948
National League Division Three

Coventry	(H)	58-24	54-30
Coventry	(A)	45-37	36-48
Cradley Heath	(H)	43-40	58-26
Cradley Heath	(A)	30-54	40-44
Exeter	(H)	32-51	38-46
Exeter	(A)	25-58	43-41
Hanley	(H)	46-38	48-35
Hanley	(A)	40-44	34-50
Hastings	(H)	49-34	57-26
Hastings	(A)	29-55	40-44
Hull	(H)	59-24	51-33
Hull	(A)	26-58	26-58
Poole	(H)	48-36	57-27
Poole	(A)	46-37	28½-55½
Southampton	(H)	38-45	45-39
Southampton	(A)	34-50	36-48
Tamworth	(H)	42-42	63-21
Tamworth	(A)	24-60	36-48
Wombwell	(H)	57-27	65-19
Wombwell	(A)	36-46	31-52
Yarmouth	(H)	48-33	57-27
Yarmouth	(A)	33-51	30-51

Scorers: P. Lansdale 381, L. Read 344, P. Robinson 339, A. Gray 212, B. Waddell 157, I. Kessell 146, V. Gent 87½, T. Gibson 83, W. Matthews 50, B. Newell 36, C. Challis 13, D. Hynes 6, K. Slee 4, B. Sobey 2, B. Bundy 1.

1949
National League Division Three

Exeter	(H)	44-30	51-33
Exeter	(A)	40-44	36-47
Halifax	(H)	52-32	40-44
Halifax	(A)	29-54	26-58
Hanley	(H)	54-30	42-42
Hanley	(A)	32-52	24-60
Hastings	(H)	48-32	40-43
Hastings	(A)	31-52	42-42
Hull	(H)	59-25	–
Hull	(A)	40-44	–
Leicester	(H)	49-34	50-34
Leicester	(A)	39-45	32-52
Liverpool	(H)	54-29	50-34
Liverpool	(A)	45-39	43-41
Oxford	(H)	53-31	62-22
Oxford	(A)	43-40	51-33
Poole	(H)	35-47	41-43
Poole	(A)	46-37	35-49
Rayleigh	(H)	46-38	50-34
Rayleigh	(A)	56-27	51-33
Swindon	(H)	–	50-34
Swindon	(A)	–	47-36
Tamworth	(H)	50-34	48-36
Tamworth	(A)	27-57	33-50
Yarmouth	(H)	57-27	56-28
Yarmouth	(A)	43-41	24-58

NB. Swindon took over Hull's fixtures.

Scorers: P. Lansdale 480, L. Read 427, P. Robinson 379, G. Wall 246, A. Smith 145, J. Bradford 143, I. Kessell 141, B. Wigg 46, B. Waddell 45, G. Woodger 13, W. Matthews 13, T. Boshoff 10, T. Gibson 5, A. Peel 2, M. Jones 1.

1950
National League Division Two

Ashfield	(H)	37-47	
Ashfield	(A)	32-52	
Coventry	(H)	45-39	
Coventry	(A)	29-54	
Cradley Heath	(H)	40-44	
Cradley Heath	(A)	56-28	
Edinburgh	(H)	40-43	
Edinburgh	(A)	32-51	
Fleetwood	(H)	57-27	
Fleetwood	(A)	38-46	
Halifax	(H)	47-37	
Halifax	(A)	35-49	
Hanley	(H)	60-24	
Hanley	(A)	24-60	
Newcastle	(H)	58-26	
Newcastle	(A)	41-42	
Norwich	(H)	49-35	
Norwich	(A)	30-54	
Sheffield	(H)	60-24	
Sheffield	(A)	29-55	
Southampton	(H)	47-37	
Southampton	(A)	34-50	
Walthamstow	(H)	44-40	
Walthamstow	(A)	43-40	
Glasgow W.City	(H)	54-30	
Glasgow W.City	(A)	23-61	
Yarmouth	(H)	56-28	
Yarmouth	(A)	30-54	

Scorers: P. Lansdale 254, P. Robinson 237, L. Read 218, A. Smith 135, G. Wall 127, J. Bradford 74, B. Thatcher 56, C. Bailey 39, D. Hayles 18, W. Mawdsley 11, G. Woodger 1, B. Wigg 0, B. Slade 0.

1951
National League Division Three

Aldershot	(H)	53-31	42-42
Aldershot	(A)	30-54	31-53
Cardiff	(H)	51-33	54-30
Cardiff	(A)	36-48	41-43
Exeter	(H)	41-42	35-49
Exeter	(A)	30-54	31-53
Long Eaton	(H)	65-19	59-25
Long Eaton	(A)	39-45	40-42
Poole	(H)	36-48	43-40
Poole	(A)	30-54	33-51
Rayleigh	(H)	44-40	40-44
Rayleigh	(A)	27-57	33-50
St Austell	(H)	44-40	53-31
St Austell	(A)	48-36	46-38
Swindon	(H)	37-47	47-37
Swindon	(A)	32-52	39-44
Wolverhampton	(H)	61-23	51-33
Wolverhampton	(A)	50-34	48-36

Scorers: A. Smith 368, G. Wall 317, B. Hitchcock 182, B. Thatcher 138, J. Bradford 123, R. Barrett 94, G. Craig 93, F. Wheeler 78, D. Hayles 29, D. Fursey 23, T. Turnham 21, F. Holcombe 19, G. Watts 18, R. Wainwright 17, T. Lockyer 0, V. Thyer 0.

1952
Southern League

Aldershot	(H)	46-37	64-20
Aldershot	(A)	42-42	39-45
Cardiff	(H)	53-31	51-33
Cardiff	(A)	37-47	22-58
Exeter	(H)	57-27	40-44
Exeter	(A)	40-44	35-48
Ipswich	(H)	58-25	57-26
Ipswich	(A)	49-35	52-32
Long Eaton	(H)	64-20	★
Long Eaton	(A)	33-51	★
Rayleigh	(H)	45-39	26-58
Rayleigh	(A)	39-45	39-44
St Austell	(H)	53-31	59-25
St Austell	(A)	38-45	45-39
Southampton	(H)	59-25	58-26
Southampton	(A)	35-49	40-44
Swindon	(H)	59-25	44-39
Swindon	(A)	43-41	30-54
Wolverhampton	(H)	45-39	55-29
Wolverhampton	(A)	31-51	25-59

★ Long Eaton resigned from league.

Scorers: A. Smith 360, G. Wall 355, B. Thatcher 254, P. Lansdale 193, B. Hitchcock 133, T. Stevens 96, D. Fursey 75, F. Wheeler 68, R. Moreton 33, B. Rundle 20, J. Bradford 14, D. Hayles 5, A. Dabinett 4.

1953
Southern League

Cardiff	(H)	49-35	★
Cardiff	(A)	31-53	★
Exeter	(H)	41-43	36-48
Exeter	(A)	25-59	33-51
Ipswich	(H)	48-36	51-33
Ipswich	(A)	35-48	35-49
Oxford	(H)	44-40	49-35
Oxford	(A)	33-50	39-45
Rayleigh	(H)	38-46	38-46
Rayleigh	(A)	32-52	33-51
St Austell	(H)	37-47	46-38
St Austell	(A)	52-32	37-47
Southampton	(H)	47-37	38-45
Southampton	(A)	36-47	31-51
Swindon	(H)	42-42	41-43
Swindon	(A)	35-49	38-46

★ Cardiff resigned from league.

Scorers: A. Smith 255, P. Lansdale 221, B. Thatcher 179, L. Read 124, G. Wall 110, S. Clark 51, K. Hayden 40, D. Timms 33, D. Fursey 19, D. Harris 12, D. Howard 10, B. Hitchcock 10, J. Sargeant 6, J. Hillard 6, J. Bridson 5, S. Bedford 4, J. Summers 2, F. Wheeler 2, T. Lewis 0, V. Thyer 0.

1954
Southern Shield/National League Division Two

Bristol	(H)	36-48 /	–
Bristol	(A)	29-55 /	–
Exeter	(H)	43-41 /	–
Exeter	(A)	28-55 /	–
Oxford	(H)	51-33 /	–
Oxford	(A)	31-53 /	–
Poole	(H)	Not run	
Poole	(A)	20-64 /	–
Southampton	(H)	44-39 /	49-35
Southampton	(A)	40-44 /	–
Swindon	(H)	31-53 /	–
Swindon	(A)	22-61 /	–
Coventry	(A)	★ /	30-54

★ Coventry did not compete in the Southern Shield.

Plymouth resigned from the league after two matches.

Scorers (Shield and League): A. Smith 118, P. Lansdale 101, B. Thatcher 66, H. Bull 48, H. Mayhead 43, G. Wall 35, K. Holmes 32, K. Hayden 24, V. Gent 19, K. Bock 15, J. Gates 15, D. Harris 2.

1961
Provincial League

Cradley Heath	(H)	54-24
Cradley Heath	(A)	38-40
Edinburgh	(H)	46-32
Edinburgh	(A)	32-46
Exeter	(H)	44-34
Exeter	(A)	36-41
Middlesbrough	(H)	47-31
Middlesbrough	(A)	37-40
Newcastle	(H)	48-30
Newcastle	(A)	33-44
Poole	(H)	40-38
Poole	(A)	37-39
Rayleigh	(H)	45-32
Rayleigh	(A)	37-41
Sheffield	(H)	47-31
Sheffield	(A)	41-37
Stoke	(H)	41-36
Stoke	(A)	26-51
Wolverhampton	(H)	44-34
Wolverhampton	(A)	53-25

Scorers: J. Scott 212, C. Cox 158, M. Mattingley 141, R. Bagley 119, C. Julian 94, P. Flanagan 39, R. Wickett 31, C. Blewett 23, G. Summers 4, E. Baker 2, F. Evans 2, R. Dent 1, C. Thomas 0.

1962
Provincial League

Bradford	(H)	44-34
Bradford	(A)	36-42
Cradley Heath	(H)	45-33
Cradley Heath	(A)	29-49
Edinburgh	(H)	39-39
Edinburgh	(A)	39-38
Exeter	(H)	42-36
Exeter	(A)	34-44
Leicester	(H)	41-37
Leicester	(A)	46-32
Middlesbrough	(H)	46-32
Middlesbrough	(A)	29-49
Neath	(H)	39-39
Neath	(A)	31-47
Newcastle	(H)	38-37
Newcastle	(A)	29-47
Poole	(H)	43-34
Poole	(A)	32-45
Sheffield	(H)	42-36
Sheffield	(A)	23-54
Stoke	(H)	53-25
Stoke	(A)	36-41
Wolverhampton	(H)	55-22
Wolverhampton	(A)	28-50

Scorers: J. Squibb 234, C. Cox 206, C. Julian 158, C. Blewett 122, M. Mattingley 69, B. Roger 36, I. Toms 35, G. Summers 27, L. Philp 5, R. Harris 4, F. Bettis 3, D. Collins 2, J. Swales 1, G. Penniket 0.

1968
British League Division Two

Belle Vue Colts	(H)	43-35
Belle Vue Colts	(A)	30-48
Berwick	(H)	43-35
Berwick	(A)	41-37
Canterbury	(H)	47-31
Canterbury	(A)	35-43
Crayford	(H)	54-24
Crayford	(A)	27-51
Middlesbrough	(H)	53-25
Middlesbrough	(A)	31-47
Nelson	(H)	50-28
Nelson	(A)	21-55
Rayleigh	(H)	48-30
Rayleigh	(A)	34-40
Reading	(H)	42-36
Reading	(A)	28-50
Weymouth	(H)	41-36
Weymouth	(A)	36-42

Scorers:
M. Cake 187, C. Bass 101, T. George 98, D. Whitaker 97, P. Woodcock 96, C. Roynon 48, F. Payne 32, K. Marks 31, I. Gills 24, B. Coles 10, D. Jewell 5, E. Howe 2, M. Gimlett 0.

1969
British League Division Two

Belle Vue Colts	(H)	36-42
Belle Vue Colts	(A)	20-57
Berwick	(H)	34-44
Berwick	(A)	22-55
Canterbury	(H)	40-38
Canterbury	(A)	26-52
Crayford	(H)	40-38
Crayford	(A)	21-56
Crewe	(H)	49-28
Crewe	(A)	17-61
Doncaster	(H)	37-40
Doncaster	(A)	27-51
Eastbourne	(H)	38-40
Eastbourne	(A)	30-47
Ipswich	(H)	42-35
Ipswich	(A)	21-57
King's Lynn	(H)	35-42
King's Lynn	(A)	31-46
Long Eaton	(H)	51-27
Long Eaton	(A)	35-38
Middlesbrough	(H)	45-33
Middlesbrough	(A)	24-54
Nelson	(H)	55-23
Nelson	(A)	35-43
Rayleigh	(H)	49-29
Rayleigh	(A)	21-57
Reading	(H)	42-36
Reading	(A)	21-51
Romford	(H)	36-39
Romford	(A)	20-58

Scorers: C. Sanders 236, B. Coles 187, D. Whitaker 176, C. Roynon 149, K. Marks 77, J. Hammond 69, I. Gills 32, J. Ellis 19, C. Cox 18, C. Facey 16, F. Payne 12, T. Smith 8, P. Arnold 5, P. Sly 3, S. Wallace 2, R. Skinner 1, A. Degan 0.

Other titles published by Tempus

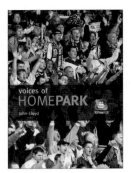

Voices of Home Park
JOHN LLOYD

These are the voices of Home Park – stories and memories from fans who have followed Argyle through thick and thin down the years, through promotions and relegations, epic cup runs and crushing defeats; the strange and sometimes hilarious events that have marked Argyle's hundred years as a professional club.

0 7524 2949 3

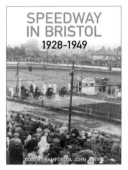

Speedway in Bristol 1928-1949
ROBERT BAMFORD & JOHN JARVIS

Speedway first came to Bristol in 1928 at the Knowle Stadium. The first period of racing came to an end in 1930, but the sport returned in 1936, when the club acquired the nickname 'Bulldogs'. For a while Bristol were the best supported team in the Provincial League, also spending a season in the top division before the war. After hostilities ceased, another terrific promotion to Division One was achieved in 1949. This is the definitive history of Bristol Speedway up to that time.

0 7524 3788 7

Southampton Speedway
PAUL EUSTACE

This collection of team groups, action photographs, portraits and other memorabilia, compiled by Paul Eustace, charts the history of speedway at Banister Court Stadium from the pioneer days of 1928 to its sad demise in 1963. Many of speedway's biggest names wore the Saints' race jacket: Sprouts Elder, Jack and Norman Parker, Split Waterman, Bjorn Knutsson and Barry Briggs brought thrills to thousands at Banister Court, as did many local favourites who are also featured.

0 7524 2433 5

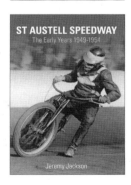

St Austell Speedway The Early Years 1949-1954
JEREMY JACKSON

Post-war Cornish speedway centered on Cornish Stadium at Par Moor, home of St Austell Speedway from 1950 onwards. Although the Gulls did not challenge for honours in their early years, huge crowds and legendary riders came to the track as speedway became an important part of life in post-war Cornwall. In this book, containing many rare photographs of St Austell's speedway legends, Cornish speedway writer Jeremy Jackson recalls the formative years of the shale sport west of the Tamar river.

0 7524 3789 5

If you are interested in purchasing other books published by Tempus, or in case you have difficulty finding any Tempus books in your local bookshop, you can also place orders directly through our website

www.tempus-publishing.com